International Market Linkages and U.S. Manufacturing: Prices, Profits, and Patterns

International Market Linkages and U.S. Manufacturing: Prices, Profits, and Patterns

Thomas A. Pugel
New York University
Graduate School of
Business Administration

Ballinger Publishing Company • Cambridge, Massachusetts
A Subsidiary of Harper & Row, Publishers, Inc.

iv

048347

International Standard Book Number: 0-88410-490-7

Library of Congress Catalog Card Number: 78-24108

Printed in the United States of America

Library of Congress Cataloging in Publication Data

Pugel, Thomas A.
  International market linkages and U.S. manufacturing.

  Bibliography: p.
  1. United States—Commercial policy. 2. International economic relations. I. Title.
HF1455.P84   382'.3   78-24108
ISBN 0-88410-490-7

HF
1455
.P84
1978

Contents

List of Figures

List of Tables

x

Preface

The United States, although a large economy, is not an economic island. Its interdependence with the rest of the world has become increasingly important and apparent over the last decade. I offer this modest work to further the understanding of the United States in the world economy.

I am most grateful for the patience and editorial skill of my wife, Bonnie, and for the understanding and support of my parents, Mr. and Mrs. Edmund A. Pugel. I thank especially Richard E. Caves for encouragement and helpful comments. I also thank Rachel McCulloch, Thomas Horst, Michael E. Porter, Thomas Stoker, Ronald Saunders, Kurt Brown, Peter Jarrett, Thomas Barthold, James Linfield, and Bronwyn Hall for comments and assistance. I express gratitude to my final draft typist, Carolyn Pearson, and to my typist on previous drafts, Rebecca Wentworth.

I am grateful to the U.S. Department of Labor, Bureau of International Labor Affairs, for generous financial support of previous research by the author on related topics. Of course, the views expressed here do not necessarily reflect those of the Department.

Thomas A. Pugel

Cambridge, Mass.
August 1978

International Market Linkages and U.S. Manufacturing: Prices, Profits, and Patterns

Chapter 1

Introduction

Over the last fifteen years international trade of the United States has increased in importance to many domestic manufacturing industries and to the economy in general. In 1960, the percentage of total U.S. sales of manufactured goods that were exports was 3.6 percent.[1] In 1965, this percentage was little changed at 3.5 percent. In 1967 this percentage began to grow, increasing to 4.1 percent in 1970 and 6.7 percent in 1975.

Over the same period imported manufactured goods also increased in importance to domestic consumers. In 1960 the ratio of imported manufactured goods to exported manufactures was 54.5 percent.[2] This percentage was relatively constant until 1964. In 1965 it rose to 64.5 percent. By 1970 it was 88.3 percent. The ratio was greater than 100 percent in each of 1972 and 1973. As exports became more important to domestic manufacturers, the significance of imported manufactured goods to domestic consumers also increased. The international payments surplus in manufactured goods that the United States had enjoyed since World War II was reduced and eventually reversed.

In 1960 the ratio of U.S. outward foreign direct investment to gross domestic nonresidential fixed investment was 4.2 percent.[3] Although this ratio is more erratic than either of the trade ratios, it was 7.0 percent in 1965 and 7.3 percent in 1970. Between 1973 and 1975 it remained at about 10 percent.

Exports, imports, and outward foreign direct investment have each grown in importance to the U.S. economy over the last fifteen years. This book attempts to analyze the underlying determinants of U.S. international trade and investment activity in manufactures and to analyze the effects of international trade and investment on prices and profitability in U.S. manufacturing industries. The book presents an empirical analysis of a number of hypotheses concerning the interrelations among market structure, market conduct, international trade, and international investment across these industries.

One focus of the book is the effect of international trade on the pricing behavior and profitability of U.S. manufacturing firms. The book demonstrates empirically that import competition improves the allocative performance of less competitive domestic industries by constraining their pricing behavior. Domestic consumers benefit not only from the availability of imports but also from the lower prices of their domestic substitutes. This improvement in allocative efficiency is a source of gains from international trade in addition to the gains demonstrated in analyses that assume perfect competition in all markets.

The book demonstrates that the ability to export tends to enhance the profitability of U.S. firms. U.S. comparative advantage is shown to be directly related to the use of skilled labor in production, especially the use of scientists and engineers in research and development (R & D) activity. A theory of pricing of U.S. exports is based on these observations. U.S. firms are able to exploit their comparative advantage in newer, technically sophisticated products by charging higher export prices. Although R & D is shown not to be a barrier to entry into production in the United States, the availability of skilled labor may be an important barrier in foreign markets that exhibit lower mobility of technical personnel. Thus, while domestic pricing is constrained by the competition of smaller U.S. firms, the larger U.S. firms face less severe competition in foreign markets.

A second focus of the book is the analysis of the determinants of the commodity pattern of U.S. trade in manufactures and of outward foreign direct investment across manufacturing industries. In addition to comparative advantage, transportability, and government import policy, the influence of market structure and market conduct on the trade pattern is explored. Advertising, which is shown to act as a barrier to the entry of domestic firms, is found also to act as a barrier to trade.

Domestic pricing is expected to influence the pattern of trade. If domestic price is elevated over cost, an incentive to foreign firms to export to the United States is created in addition to any foreign comparative advantage. The effect of pricing on imports could not be demonstrated using ordinary least-squares estimation.

In the relations between domestic pricing and imports, a simultaneity of hypotheses is evident. Import competition is hypothesized to constrain domestic pricing, but pricing acts as an incentive to import. In the presence of simultaneity, ordinary least squares is a biased estimation technique. A third focus of the book is the development of a structural model of U.S. manufacturing industry that is estimated by using a consistent statistical technique.

METHOD OF ANALYSIS AND DATA

The method of analysis is a cross-sectional analysis of U.S. manufacturing industries assuming long-run equilibrium for most relations. Ordinary least-squares estimates of hypothesized relations are presented in conjunction with the discussions of the determinants of profitability, trade patterns, foreign direct investment (FDI), advertising, and producer concentration. Because ordinary least-squares estimates arc likely to be biased, the equations of the model are reestimated by two-stage least squares.

The study utilizes seventy-one of seventy-six IRS minor industries defined as of 1968. Five industries are omitted from the sample:

—Sugar (IRS 2060) is dropped due to the many nontariff trade barriers, especially quotas, that affect this industry.[4]
—Chemicals and Allied Products Not Allocable (IRS 2899) is omitted because it is a very small residual industry without a Standard Industrial Classification (SIC) counterpart.
—Petroleum Refining (IRS 2910) is dropped for a number of reasons, including the import quota, extensive use of depletion allowances by integrated producers, and the predilection of petroleum multinational corporations to show much of their profit at the foreign crude extraction stage of production to take advantage of U.S. tax law during this period.[5]
—Ordnance (IRS 3930) is dropped because much of its output is sold to the United States and other governments. This market is likely to work differently from markets in which private transactions predominate.
—Miscellaneous Manufactured Products (IRS 3990) is omitted because it is too miscellaneous, covering all of SIC 2-digit industry 39.

IRS minor industries correspond to about the 3-digit level of the SIC. Industries are reasonably well defined at this level although some may be too aggregated. Data limitations preclude a full analysis at a more detailed level of industry classification.

Data are obtained from a variety of sources. Much data come from five major U.S. data sources: *IRS Sourcebook Statistics of Income*

Corporations, Census of Manufactures, Annual Survey of Manufactures, U.S. Commodity Exports and Imports as Related to Output, and *Census of Population.* These data are reported on the basis of three methods of industrial classification: the IRS minor industries, the SIC, and the Census of Population detailed industries. The concordances among these classification systems are generally good and are presented in Table A-3 for the seventy-one industries used in this study.

A serious concordance problem is encountered for two variables reported according to the Standard International Trade Classification (SITC). The two variables are the fraction of U.S. imports affected by nontariff barriers to trade[6] and U.S. effective tariff rates.[7]

Where possible variables are measured as averages over the four years 1967 to 1970. Averages should lessen any short-run deviations or disturbances in the data and justify in part the assumption of long-run equilibrium.

AN OUTLINE OF THE BOOK

Chapters 2 through 4 of this book present hypotheses and statistical analysis. Chapters 2 and 3 examine domestic pricing and international trade patterns, respectively, using ordinary least squares. Chapter 4 develops additional equations of the structural model, equations explaining outward FDI, advertising, and producer concentration. Chapter 4 also presents estimation of the full structural model. Chapter 5 explores the policy implications of the results. A summary of each chapter is now presented.

Chapter 2 develops a model of pricing and profitability of U.S. manufacturing industry. The model is based on a barriers to entry limit-pricing theory. The chapter extends previous work in two directions. First, international influences are considered within the model. Second, the interaction of domestic entry barriers, international market linkages, and domestic producer competition is recognized explicitly in the model and the statistical analysis. The major findings of the chapter are that import competition constrains pricing in domestic industries that otherwise have market power but that tariffs reduce the constraint in these industries. Statistical support is found for the interactive hypothesis. A theory of price-discriminating U.S. exporters is presented.

Chapter 3 develops and tests a model of international trade patterns. The model includes comparative advantage theories of trade, the effects of domestic market structure and conduct on trade patterns, and the role of frictions based on both transport cost and government import policy. One aspect of market conduct, advertising, is found to alter trade patterns in that advertising acts as a barrier to trade. The Heckscher-Ohlin theories of comparative advantage and the product life-cycle theory receive statistical support. The conclusion is that these theories should be considered complementary in explaining the U.S. pattern of trade in manufactured goods.

Chapter 4 explores the determinants of U.S. outward FDI. In concluding the consideration of the interrelationships among structure, conduct, trade, and FDI, the study demonstrates empirical support for market structure and conduct determinants of FDI. The relation of FDI to exports or imports could not be demonstrated statistically.

After developing two additional equations, the advertising and concentration equations, a two-stage least-squares estimation of structural models of U.S. manufacturing industry is presented. Two-stage least-squares estimates are preferred for their consistency. In a number of instances, ordinary least squares are found to be biased although most estimates are essentially unchanged.

The book concludes by examining policy implications in Chapter 5. Two policy implications follow from the analysis. Because import competition is significant in constraining domestic pricing in relatively concentrated industries, these industries should be opened to increased import competition through lowering of tariffs, elimination of quotas, and removal of other nontariff barriers to trade in order to improve the allocative efficiency of these industries. The results also indicate that any movement toward a more protectionist stand in U.S. commercial policy is likely to cause an increase in prices relative to costs in addition to, and perhaps instead of, expansion of domestic output and employment in less competitive industries.

A second policy implication follows from statistical support for the tacit collusion or shared monopoly hypothesis. This support is demonstrated in the interactive effect of domestic producer concentration on the determination of prices. Antitrust action aimed at reducing producer concentration is likely to improve allocative efficiency in the economy even if other aspects of market structure and conduct cannot be altered. New antitrust laws allowing greater weight to be placed on structural aspects of an industry may be desirable. Antitrust action should, however, continue on an individual case basis. Producer concentration is likely to lead to allocative inefficiency in pricing, but pricing is only one aspect of market performance. This book does not present analysis of technical efficiency and technological progressiveness, both of which may be adversely affected by imposed deconcentration.

NOTES

1. Export data from *Economic Report of the President,* 1977, Table B-96. Manufactured good sales from *Economic Report of the President,* 1977, Table B-81.

2. Export and import data from *Economic Report of the President,* 1977, Table B-96. The export data is reported f.a.s. The import data is reported at customs value.

3. Foreign direct investment data from *International Economic Report of the President,* 1977, Table 46. Gross domestic nonresidential fixed investment from *Economic Report of the President,* 1977, Table B-14.

4. I. Mintz, *U.S. Import Quotas: Costs and Consequences,* 1973, analyzes the economic effects of sugar quotas. D.J. Gerber, "The United States Sugar Quota Program: A Study in the Direct Congressional Control of Imports," *Journal of Law and Economics,* April 1976, traces the legislative history of these quotas.

5. For a discussion of these issues, see J.M. Blair, *The Control of Oil,* 1976. K.W. Dam, "Implementation of Import Quotas: The Case of Oil," *Journal of Law and Economics,* April 1971, discusses the history of the oil quota.

6. I. Walter, "Non-Tariff Protection Among Industrial Countries: Some Preliminary Evidence," *Economia Internazionale,* May 1972.

7. R.E. Baldwin, *Non-Tariff Distortions of International Trade,* 1970.

Chapter 2

Domestic Prices and Profits

The long-run equilibrium relation between prices and costs, in addition to its direct relation to firm and industry profitability, is important to domestic household consumers, who allocate a limited budget among alternative goods and services, and to domestic producers, who purchase material inputs and investment goods. This chapter analyzes the equilibrium relation between prices and costs in U.S. manufacturing industry by examining modified price-cost margins, defined as unit after-tax receipts minus unit cost all divided by unit price.

The major goal of this chapter is analyzing pricing across industries. Purchasers are interested in prices as low as possible, the microeconomic condition that price equals marginal cost for each good. Producers, however, strive to elevate their prices over cost to increase profits. In long-run equilibrium the firms' ability to do so depends on industry barriers to entry, which prevent an influx of new sellers drawn by the relatively higher rates of profit, and on recognition that the firms in the industry are interdependent and should mutually constrain their competitive actions.

This chapter extends most previous analysis of this equilibrium relation to include the impact of international trade and investment. In some industries import penetration offers significant competition to domestic producers, constraining their pricing. Barriers to import therefore form an important part of the domestic market structure. Exporting and foreign direct investment allow domestic producers access to additional markets.

A central assumption is that costs are minimized for all but the smallest U.S. firms. Because the United States offers a large market domestically, U.S. producers utilize plants of optimal or near-optimal size for all but "fringe" production.[1] Other costs are expended only as optimal for profit enhancement.[2] In studying other smaller economies cost-minimizing production efficiency may not be an appropriate assumption,[3] but for the United States it may be reasonable.

The statistical analysis of this chapter presents strong support for an interactive domestic barriers-international trade-domestic producer concentration model of pricing behavior in manufacturing industries. Two policy implications follow from these results. First, antitrust actions aimed at lowering domestic concentration are likely to lower domestic prices as long as production efficiency is not impaired. Second, even without antitrust actions, pricing in domestically concentrated industries can be restrained by additional foreign competition created by lowering tariffs and eliminating any quotas or other non-tariff barriers to import.

DOMESTIC ENTRY BARRIERS

Neoclassical economic theory concludes that, assuming constant costs of production over the relevant range for each industry, in long-run equilibrium the rate of return on capital is equalized across industries. This rate of return is the opportunity cost of capital. Price equals marginal cost in each industry. If the rate of return is r, the relationship can be presented as

$$\frac{\text{Profit}}{\text{Sales}} = r \, \frac{\text{Capital}}{\text{Sales}} \qquad (2\text{-}1)$$

The theory adds one qualification in the presence of uncertainty. The rate of return that is equalized is a risk-adjusted rate of return. Risk varies across industries. Unfortunately, this risk is an ex ante concept for which empirical testing is difficult.[4]

We do not observe a complete equalization of rates of return across industries. Violations of neoclassical assumptions may explain this variance if risk differentials do not.[5] The crucial assumptions of neoclassical theory are a large number of firms, which makes collusion of any sort difficult among the firms in the industry, and ease of entry and exit, which allows mobility of firms in the face of differing profit opportunities across industries. These two assumptions are inter-related. Violation leads to a theory of market imperfections known as "barriers to entry," pioneered by J.S. Bain.[6] This theory is incorporated into the market structure-conduct-performance paradigm of industrial organization.[7]

The technology of the industry may create entry barriers. Minimum efficient scale of plant (MES), defined as the smallest output for which the long-run average or unit cost of production reaches a minimum, is the most important aspect of market structure given by technology. The larger is the minimum efficient scale of plant relative to the size of the market, the more difficult is entry. If MES is large relative to the market, the large increase in output accompanying entry at efficient scale severely disrupts the market, driving down prices and profits. Entry at suboptimal scale to avoid disruption incurs higher unit costs of production. Bain referred to this entry barrier as the scale economy advantages of established firms. Because new entrants face this disadvantage, established firms can raise price over cost without inducing entry. The maximum price that can be set without inducing entry is known as the limit price.[8] This limit price depends not only on the ratio of MES to market size, but also on the extent of cost disadvantage of smaller scale production. A limit-price model is presented in the next section.

The capital requirement for entry at efficient scale, defined as the investment necessary to enter an industry producing at the minimum efficient scale of plant, is another barrier to entry. The uncertainty associated with entry creates a risk premium in lending to a new entrant. This premium may be larger than the premium paid by firms already established. In addition, new entrants incur higher transaction costs in that lenders need to gather information about the relatively less known entrant. In these ways firms now in the industry enjoy an absolute capital cost advantage over new entrants. The advantage can be stated on a limit-price basis.[9]

Bain suggests that there are forms of absolute cost barriers to entry in addition to capital cost disadvantages.[10] Firms holding patents on production processes or other knowledge not freely disseminated have an absolute cost advantage over their less efficient rivals. Firms holding superior raw material source rights also have an absolute cost advantage. These differences in firm costs naturally generate the flow of entry, growth, decline, and exit of firms in an industry through the competitive process. But if these differences are used by firms in an industry to impede entry of new firms, the competitive process is blocked. Prices can be systematically elevated above marginal cost in long-run equilibrium.

Product differentiation is a third source of barriers to entry.[11] Differentiation partially isolates each firm from the actions of other firms. As product differentiation increases, the own-price elasticity of demand for each firm's product decreases.

New entrants face a number of constraints related to differentiation. New entrants may be at an absolute cost disadvantage. Entrants must overcome both habits developed through experience with established products and, if advertising is the primary vehicle for establishing and maintaining a branded product, the noise already in the market for information. Entry requires either relatively large advertising outlays, at least initially, or accepting a lower price to encourage a first purchase of the new product. Entrants often face a capital cost constraint as well because of relatively high risk premiums in borrowing. The investment in creating the intangible asset of a differentiated product is especially risky and may have very low salvage value if the attempt fails. Scale economies in advertising, whether caused by a decreasing cost per message as the number of messages increases or by an increasing effectiveness per message as the number of messages increases, present the entrant with the same dilemma faced in our discussion of technological scale barriers. These absolute cost and scale economy aspects of the product differentiation-advertising barrier can be combined into an analysis that again indicates that a limit-pricing policy by established firms yields a long-run equilibrium with excess profit.[12]

The entry barriers theory establishes the possibility of long-run excess profits varying across industries according to the incidence of the barriers. Whether the excess profits are realized in any one industry depends on the state of competition among firms within the industry. If firms act as pure competitors, ignoring the reactions of rivals to their own actions, excess profits are not likely as price is driven down to cost. If firms realize their mutual interdependence, they circumscribe their competitive actions. At least a part of the potential excess of price over cost is realized. The number of firms and their relative sizes are important in determining the extent to which mutual interdependence is recognized. A measure of domestic producer concentration is used to represent the state of domestic producer competition.[13]

Over any time period some industries are not in long-run equilibrium. A likely disequilibrium is that the industry is growing faster or slower than firms in the industry (and potential entrants) expect. In either of these cases, investment plans and capacity are not correctly adjusted to demand growth, creating short-run pricing pressures. Expectations are not quantified easily, but actual growth is included in the empirical analysis in the hope that it correlates with the difference between realized and expected growth.

The pricing model developed so far, omitting risk adjustment since risk is not easily analyzed empirically, is summarized:

$$\frac{\text{Profit}}{\text{Sales}} = r \frac{\text{Capital}}{\text{Sales}} + f(\text{MES/Market, Capital}$$
Requirements, Advertising
Intensity, C4, Growth) $\qquad$ (2-2)

Advertising intensity measures at least one aspect of the product differentiation barrier. The concentration measure is the four-firm concentration ratio. A number of investigators have used this model or a similar model to analyze pricing and profitability across U.S. manufacturing industries.[14] The model implicitly assumes that the United States is a closed economy. A few investigators have analyzed the impact of international factors on U.S. manufacturing.[15] The next three sections present discussion of the effects of import competition, export opportunity, and foreign direct investment on pricing and profitability.

IMPORT COMPETITION

Imports are an additional source of competition in the domestic market. Import competition may compel domestic producers to modify their pricing behavior. The influence of import competition on domestic price and profitability can be demonstrated in formal models of a domestic monopolist facing import competition. The first model is an absolute cost disadvantage pricing model in which the least disadvantaged potential entrants are foreign firms as exporters. The second model extends this analysis to demonstrate the importance of the elasticity of import supply.

Consider a monopolist with constant costs of production and a given domestic demand. Let import supply be perfectly elastic at a foreign received price p_F. In notation,

$$Q_D = f(p), f' < 0 \qquad (2\text{-}3)$$

$$MC = c \qquad (2\text{-}4)$$

$$p_M = (l + t)p_F + T \qquad (2\text{-}5)$$

where Q_D is domestic demand, p is domestic price, MC is marginal cost of domestic production, p_M is the domestic selling price of imports, t is the domestic tariff rate, and T is unit freight and insurance cost.

In the absence of import competition, the monopolist sets marginal revenue equal to marginal cost:

$$p + \frac{f}{f'} = c \qquad (2\text{-}6)$$

or

$$p = -\frac{f}{f'} + c \tag{2-7}$$

However, if $(-[f/f'] + c)$ exceeds p_M, the monopolist's pricing is constrained because p_M sets a ceiling on domestic prices.[16] In notation,

$$p = \begin{cases} -\dfrac{f}{f'} + c & \text{if} \quad -\dfrac{f}{f'} + c < p_M \\[4mm] p_M & \text{if} \quad -\dfrac{f}{f'} + c \geqslant p_M \end{cases} \tag{2-8}$$

This result indicates important elements of the pricing constraint. Given c and $f(p)$, the constraint is more severe the lower the p_F, t, and T. The constraint of import competition is related to foreign received price, foreign costs through this relation, the domestic tariff rate, and the ease of transportability of the product. However, the import share Q_M/Q_D is indeterminate at price p_M and is likely to be zero as the monopolist generally sets a price slightly below p_M.

This model illustrates the concept of absolute cost disadvantage limit pricing. The selling price of imports, p_M, is above the production cost of the established producer, c. Unless demand is sufficiently elastic, the domestic producer prices above cost to the full extent of the cost disadvantage of potential entrants, setting a limit price that does not induce entry. In this instance, foreign firms are the least disadvantaged potential entrants because we assume that any price up to p_M does not induce domestic entry. Foreign firms may be favored entrants in that they are not disadvantaged by scale economies and capital requirements, because these firms are already established abroad.[17] However, the absolute cost disadvantage of foreign firms is increased by tariffs and transport costs.

Import supply need not be perfectly elastic. Let domestic demand and domestic production costs be as before. Now consider that either or both costs p_F and T may vary. These variations may result from limited supply available from each foreign country, varying production costs across these countries, and varying transport costs between each of these countries and the domestic market. For a given t, each incremental import quantity minimizes its landed price p_M, given the distribution of p_F (related to the distribution of production cost) and T. In notation,

$$Q_M = g(p_M), g' > 0 \tag{2-9}$$

where Q_M is the import supply. This formulation corresponds to the large country analysis of Heckscher-Ohlin models of international trade. Note that because U.S. tariffs are typically levied on foreign port price rather than landed cost, import supply is not efficiently determined. For a given quantity of imports, $((1 + t)p_F + T)$ is minimized rather than the economic opportunity cost of imports $(p_F + T)$. In the determination of import supply, greater weight is given to foreign production cost and less to transport cost than is economically efficient.

The domestic monopolist maximizes profit given production cost and residual demand $Q_D - Q_M$:

$$\text{Max } p \cdot (Q_D - Q_M) - c \cdot (Q_D - Q_M) \qquad (2\text{-}10)$$

Because imports are perfect substitutes for domestically produced goods, $p_M = p$ in equilibrium. Maximizing monopolist profit,

$$p + \frac{\partial p}{\partial (Q_D - Q_M)} (Q_D - Q_M) = c \qquad (2\text{-}11)$$

or

$$p = -\frac{f - g}{f' - g'} + c \qquad (2\text{-}12)$$

The price-cost margin for the domestic monopolist is

$$\frac{p - c}{p} = \frac{-(f - g)}{p} \frac{1}{(f' - g')} \qquad (2\text{-}13)$$

which equals one over the (positive) price elasticity of residual demand. This relation is also shown as

$$\frac{p - c}{p} = \frac{1 - g/f}{-\dfrac{pf'}{f} + \dfrac{g}{f}\dfrac{pg'}{g}} \qquad (2\text{-}14)$$

Let the price elasticity of domestic demand be ϵ_D and the price elasticity of import supply be ϵ_M. Then Equation 2-14 may be rewritten as

$$\frac{p - c}{p} = \frac{1 - g/f}{\epsilon_D + \dfrac{g}{f}\epsilon_M} \qquad (2\text{-}15)$$

The domestic price-cost margin is a negative function of the elasticity of import supply, other things being equal. As the import supply elasticity approaches infinity, the first model is obtained as a special case.

If the ϵ_D and ϵ_M are held constant, the price-cost margin is a negative function of the import share g/f.

$$\frac{\partial \left(\frac{p-c}{p} \right)}{\partial (g/f)} = \frac{-(\epsilon_D + \frac{g}{f}\epsilon_M) - \epsilon_M \left(1 - \frac{g}{f}\right)}{\left(\epsilon_D + \frac{g}{f}\epsilon_M\right)^2} = \frac{-(\epsilon_D + \epsilon_M)}{\left(\epsilon_D + \frac{g}{f}\epsilon_M\right)^2} \qquad (2\text{-}16)$$

This model demonstrates that the constraint placed by imports on domestic pricing is a function of the actual import share and of the elasticity of import supply.

The theory suggests that domestic demand elasticities, import supply elasticities, and the import share are significant in determining the constraint of import competition on domestic pricing. The elasticities are unobservable. The import share should capture at least part of the pricing constraint imposed by import competition. This effect is demonstrated directly in the second model. Its importance is suggested indirectly in the first model in which the constraint depends upon underlying conditions of import supply. Foreign relative costs, transport costs, and barriers to trade are shown in Chapter 3 to determine statistically import share across industries. Import share should capture the interaction of these underlying supply conditions in constraining domestic pricing across industries, assuming import supply is reasonably elastic.

The tariff rate may have additional importance to the determination of domestic price beyond any influence on the level of imports. In industries in which domestic competition does not enforce the equality of price and marginal cost, the tariff directly reduces the pricing constraint of imports. The rate may also be a focal point by which domestic price in relation to cost is set.[18] The tariff rate may be an additional government policy tool to modify domestic market performance.

Import share is also shown in Chapter 3 to reflect a number of other barriers to import, quotas among them. A quota is especially significant as a barrier to trade in the presence of domestic oligopoly or monopoly. It insulates completely the domestic market from foreign price competition once the quota is filled. In this case actual import share is not a good indicator of the constraint placed by imports on domestic pricing because the elasticity of import supply falls to zero if the quota is filled.

Although actual industries are seldom pure monopolies, the theoretical analysis indicates that import competition limits the joint profit-maximizing price that can be charged by an oligopoly. The state of producer competition determines to what extent this joint profit-maximizing solution is approached. The effect of import penetration on domestic pricing is best analyzed empirically in conjunction with the state of domestic producer competition. While import penetration may have no effect on the long-run profitability of more competitive domestic industries, it is expected to constrain pricing in the less competitive industries.

EXPORTING

In theoretical analysis the opportunity to export is shown to have a similar effect to that of import competition in restraining a domestic monopolist's pricing. The monopolist faces a more elastic world (rather than just domestic) demand curve.[19] In the limiting small country case, the monopolist becomes a price-taker. These results suggest that the distinction should be made not between import-competing and export industries, but between trade-exposed and sheltered industries.

However, a number of arguments counter these conclusions. The domestic firm may practice price discrimination. If domestic demand is less elastic than world demand, a profit-maximizing strategy charges a higher price domestically than to the rest of the world. This differential is protected by barriers to reimport. Transport costs, tariffs, and contractual arrangements or other reimport barriers prevent arbitraging between the two markets. The statistical effect of exporting on the price-cost margin may still be negative, however, if the larger domestic margin is averaged with the smaller margin on foreign sales. This averaging masks the lack of effect of exporting on domestic prices.

The bases of U.S. comparative advantage may also differentiate exporting from import competition in the determination of profitability. Export share is shown in Chapter 3 to be determined by the technological progressiveness of the industry. Exporting occurs primarily in those industries intensive in research and development. Two important implications follow from this relationship.

First, research and development (R & D) activity may act as a barrier to entry.[20] R & D shares many traits with advertising. It is a high-risk activity. Therefore, entrants may face an absolute cost disadvantage in raising capital relative to the established firms, who have demonstrated their R & D abilities. Although pervasive economies of scale have not been demonstrated for R & D activity, there appears to be a threshold scale for effective R & D expenditure. Very small firms cannot engage in competitive R & D activity due to cost disadvantages.[21] For these reasons R & D may act as an entry barrier. Its influence on price-cost margins can be estimated directly, although in its absence export share may act as an instrument for its effect in statistical analysis.

Second, the technological progressiveness of U.S. export industries may result in the production of goods without close substitutes produced by foreign firms. In this case, U.S. producers have a worldwide oligopolistic advantage. The price discrimination case discussed above may be reversed if U.S. producers exploit worldwide demand by dividing the world into separate markets. The average world price may be higher than the domestic price, and exporting enhances the observed price-cost margin.

Other considerations also suggest that exporting increases price-cost margins. Exporting allows a firm to spread its R & D and other relatively fixed costs over a larger output, thereby lowering unit cost. Domestic firms may view exporting as inherently more risky than domestic sales and demand a larger profit margin to compensate for this relatively greater risk. Exporting, by expanding the available market and reducing its average cyclical volatility, may also lead to more efficient capacity utilization.

In short, these arguments suggest that exporting increases the rewards to innovation by expanding the market for the innovation. These greater rewards may be protected from the competitive process by barriers to entry based on patents, secrecy, or capital costs. Export profits may be enhanced by the lesser antitrust restrictions on export marketing collusion among domestic producers.[22]

Because observed price-cost margins are weighted averages of the margin on domestic sales and on export sales, inclusion of export share is important in analyzing domestic firms' profitability. However, many of the above arguments suggest that exporting is not likely to affect domestic price, which, if the domestic market is segregated from the world market, is set according to the height of domestic entry barriers and the state of competition among domestic producers.

FOREIGN DIRECT INVESTMENT

Bergsten, Horst, and Moran have recently contended that U.S. foreign direct investment (FDI), based on oligopolistic advantages in large part, has feedback effects on U.S. market structure further reinforcing these markets' oligopolistic character.[23] They argue that marketing and production knowledge gained from overseas operations is transmitted back to and used in the United States, just as knowledge developed for the U.S. market is important in the decision to engage in

FDI. Vertical FDI, especially backward to foreign raw material supplies, also increases domestic absolute cost barriers to entry.

Other considerations suggest that foreign operations may increase the overall profitability of the firm although not by affecting domestic entry barriers. Overhead and other relatively fixed costs may be spread over a larger output. Cyclical fluctuations in profit may be lessened by operating in several markets. The reduction in risk may allow higher average profits to the firm. Lower taxes on foreign operations based on the use of deferral may allow higher after-tax global rates of return.

Therefore FDI may raise firm profitability although this need not be based on enhancement of domestic entry barriers as Bergsten, Horst, and Moran argue.

SPECIFICATIONS AND DATA

The model of the determination of price-cost margins across industries is summarized as:

$$\frac{\text{Profit}}{\text{Sales}} = r \frac{\text{Capital}}{\text{Sales}} + f(\text{MES/Market, Capital Requirements,}$$

Advertising Intensity, Growth, C4, Scientists & Engineers

Fraction, Import Share, Export Share, Tariff Rate, Quota,

FDI Intensity) (2-17)

The scientists and engineers fraction of total employment represents the R & D intensity of the industry.

To obtain a specification suitable for empirical analysis, Equation 2-17 is linearized. However, as argued in the first section, market performance is likely determined by the interaction of domestic entry barriers (and foreign influences) with the state of domestic producer competition. Therefore, interactive specifications are also estimated:

$$\frac{\text{Profit}}{\text{Sales}} = a + b \frac{\text{Capital}}{\text{Sales}} + b_1 (Z \cdot \text{MES/Market}) + b_2 (Z \cdot \text{Capital}$$

Requirements) $+ b_3 (Z \cdot$ Advertising Intensity$) + b_4 (Z \cdot$

Growth$) + b_5 (Z \cdot$ Scientists & Engineers Fraction$) + b_6$

$(Z \cdot$ Import Share$) + b_7 (Z \cdot$ Export Share$) + b_8 (Z \cdot$ Tariff

Rate$) + b_9 (Z \cdot$ Quota$) + b_{10} (Z \cdot$ FDI Intensity$)$ (2-18)

where Z represents the state of domestic producer competition.

The noninteractive and interactive specifications are combined in an equation of the form

$$\frac{\text{Profit}}{\text{Sales}} = a + b\,\frac{\text{Capital}}{\text{Sales}} + \sum_i (a_i + b_i Z)X_i \qquad (2\text{-}19)$$

where X_i is the ten variables MES/Market through FDI Intensity included in Equation 2-18. Results of estimation of Equation 2-19 are not presented because severe multicollinearity renders interpretation of the coefficients difficult. Hypothesis tests of the joint significance of the a_i coefficients and the b_i coefficients are presented.

Two variables are used as Z to represent the state of domestic producer competition. Each is a function of C4, which is assumed to be closely related to the state of producer competition. Each must satisfy four conditions, assuming C4 is measured decimally.

1. As C4 approaches 1.0, Z approaches 1.0.

2. As C4 approaches 0.0, Z approaches 0.0.

3. $Z > 0$, so that $\dfrac{\partial (\text{Profit/Sales})}{\partial X_i} = b_i Z \gtrless 0$ as $b_i \gtrless 0$.

4. $\dfrac{\partial Z}{\partial C4} > 0$, so that $\dfrac{\partial (\text{Profit/Sales})}{\partial C4} = \dfrac{\partial Z}{\partial C4}\sum_i b_i X_i \gtrless 0$

   as $\sum_i b_i X_i \gtrless 0$.[24]

These conditions require that the effect on profitability of entry barriers be a positive function of the level of concentration and that the effect of concentration on profitability be a positive function of entry barriers.

The first variable chosen as Z is C4 itself.[25] The second measure of Z is

$$Z = 1/[1 - \log(C4)]. \qquad (2\text{-}20)$$

This variable satisfies the four conditions:

1. As C4 approaches 1.0, $\log(C4)$ approaches 0.0, so Z approaches 1.0.
2. As C4 approaches 0.0, $\log(C4)$ approaches negative infinity, so Z approaches 0.0.

3. Since $\log(C4)$ is always negative, $Z > 0$.

4. $\dfrac{\partial Z}{\partial C4} = \dfrac{1}{C4[1 - \log(C4)]^2} > 0.$

This second representation of Z is the simplest representation utilizing $\log(C4)$ that satisfies all four conditions. It is useful in system estimation presented in Chapter 4.

The dependent variable used in this analysis is after-tax profit divided by sales. To control for variations in this ratio caused by varying capital intensity across industries, the capital-sales ratio is introduced as an independent variable. Its coefficient should equal the after-tax opportunity cost of capital. Profit and capital are entered separately in the analysis rather than using profit/capital as the dependent variable. Most analyses of the long-run effects of entry barriers on pricing, especially limit-pricing models such as those developed earlier in the third section, conclude that prices are elevated over economic unit cost according to the height of entry barriers but without relation to the capital intensity of the industry.[26] The variable profit/sales is a modified price-cost margin, gross of capital cost. Regression of profit/sales on capital/sales removes the opportunity cost of capital utilized. The remaining independent variables explain variations in

$$\frac{\text{Profit} - r\,(\text{Capital})}{\text{Sales}}$$

the after-tax excess profit margin per dollar of sales.

After-tax profits are defined as after-tax equity profits (inclusive of state and local government interest received) plus interest paid on outstanding debt. Since this amount represents the return on all assets of the firm, the measure of capital is total assets net of depreciation. After-tax profit is utilized because the theory concerns private investment decisions based upon net returns. Social return analysis would utilize pretax profits and analyze all externalities. Analysis of variations in social return across industries, even if externalities could be quantified, would include a political analysis of taxation variation across industries. This political analysis is beyond the scope of the book.

The measure of profit includes certain profit on FDI activity. The capital measure includes the book value of the parent's equity in both foreign subsidiaries and foreign branches. Biases in the data can be identified. See Appendix 4-1 for a full discussion of the FDI data and problems inherent in using it. For foreign branches the reporting of profits matches the reporting of assets so there is no systematic bias. However, for foreign subsidiaries, only after-tax repatriated foreign profits are reported, owing to deferral of taxation of unrepatriated foreign-source income. Relative to foreign subsidiary assets as reported, foreign subsidiary profits are understated. A downward bias is created in the profit to capital relationship. Inclusion of a foreign investment independent variable is likely biased negative in its relation to profitability. This bias may offset any positive effects of FDI on profitability.

The other independent variables used in the analysis are now discussed. Table A-1 provides a definition of each variable and its data sources.

MES is first measured at the 4-digit level of industrial classification. MES is defined as the average size of the largest plants producing half of the industry's output. Actual technological measures of MES are few, but the few available are well correlated with this proxy measure.[27] A shipments-weighted average of MES is computed to derive an estimate of MES at the 3-digit level. This weighted-average MES is divided by average market shipments, defined as total shipments divided by the adjusted number of markets in the continental United States, to obtain the variable MES/Market.

Weiss's method for determining the number of markets in the continental United States is used.[28] A continuous measure of transportability is obtained as the mile radius within which 80 percent of shipments are made. For industries that produce an easily transported good but face centralized demand, this radius is assumed to be 1,100 miles. A measure of the number of markets in the continental United States is obtained using the shipment radius data. This measure is adjusted to be equal to itself if the number is five or more but equal to one if the number is four or less. If the number of regional markets is two, three, or four, overlap between these markets integrates them sufficiently to generate competition at the national, rather than just the regional, level.

The capital requirement for an MES plant is obtained by multiplying the weighted-average 3-digit MES by the ratio of total assets net of depreciation to total industry shipments. The capital requirement measures the value of assets needed by a firm to enter the industry operating one MES plant.

These technologically based influences should vary in their impact on limit pricing according to the cost disadvantage of smaller scale production.[29] Therefore, alternative definitions of these variables are also used. A cost-disadvantage ratio is computed as the value added per worker in smaller plants producing half of industry output (not including plants employing ten or fewer workers) divided by value added per worker in larger plants producing the other half of industry output.[30] While this variable is not a perfect measure of total factor productivity across plant sizes,[31] it does provide one measure of the cost disadvantage of small-scale production. The cost disadvantage increases as this variable decreases. Cost-disadvantage adjusted measures of MES/Market and Capital Requirements, referred to as Cost-adjusted MES/Market and Cost-adjusted Capital Requirements, are computed as equal to zero if the cost-disadvantage ratio is greater than 0.90, indicating that smaller plants have a less than 10 percent productivity disadvantage, and as equal to their actual values if the cost-disadvantage ratio is less than or equal to 0.90, indicating a substantial productivity disadvantage to small-scale production.

The four-firm concentration ratio (C4), defined as the fraction of industry sales accounted for by the four largest firms, is used to represent the state of domestic producer competition. A number of other measures of concentration, such as the Herfindahl index or an entropy measure, could be used.[32] Investigators have found percentage measures, of which C4 is one, and other concentration measures to be highly correlated.[33] C4 is used because it is easily calculated and has been used extensively in previous research.

Concentration ratios are published at the 4-digit level of aggregation by the U.S. Census Bureau for a presumed national market. Shepherd has adjusted these ratios for both extent of geographic market and product definition.[34] For industries in which his geographic market extent does not agree with estimates provided by Weiss,[35] some readjustment is attempted. These ratios are aggregated to the 3-digit level using 4-digit industry shipments as weights to obtain C4 (4-digit).

A second estimate of C4 is obtained from the *IRS Sourcebook Statistics of Income Corporations.* For 1967, the four largest firms by assets are identified.[36] The business receipts of the four largest firms divided by total business receipts for all firms in the industry form the second four-firm concentration ratio, C4 (3-digit). No adjustment is made for geographic extent of market or product definition.

The choice between these two measures involves a number of considerations. Foremost is whether product markets (industries) are better defined at the 4-digit or 3-digit level of aggregation. Our first estimate assumes that the 4-digit level is more appropriate and aggregation is necessary only because of data limitations. The second estimate assumes that the 3-digit level is appropriate and measures C4 directly. There is no agreement on which level of classification more appropriately defines an industry.[37] Another consideration affecting the choice between these measures is that the IRS-based estimates are not adjusted for geographic extent of market. In addition, both variables suffer from measurement imprecision.

Measurement problems at the 3-digit level occur because use is made of firm data. Sales of nonprimary product output are included in the measure of business receipts. To the extent that larger firms are more diversified, the measure overstates the true level of product market concentration.

Measurement imprecision of the weighted-average 4-digit C4 occurs because of the weighting. The method of weighting is appropriate if the true model is the noninteractive model.[38] However, if the interactive model (Equation 2-18) is the true model, the method of aggregating from the 4-digit to the 3-digit level is inappropriate; in fact, there is no correct weighting method for aggregating C4 to the 3-digit level without knowledge of the 4-digit values of the variables used interactively with C4.

The scientists and engineers fraction of total employment represents the research and development intensity of an industry. At the 2-digit level of industry classification, this variable is highly correlated with R & D spending as a fraction of sales and with scientists and engineers engaged in R & D as a fraction of total employment.[39] The measure also correlates highly with the only published survey of R & D spending as a fraction of sales at the 3-digit level of classification even though this survey was taken in 1958.[40]

Import share is defined as imports divided by apparent domestic consumption. Export share is defined as exports divided by domestic shipments. FDI intensity is defined as identifiable foreign profit divided by total after-tax equity profit, used as a measure of the importance of FDI activity relative to total industry activity. This variable is discussed more fully in Appendix 4-1.

Certain barriers to import are included directly in the analysis. Both the nominal and the effective tariff rates affect the constraints imports place on domestic pricing. The nominal tariff rate is directly related to this constraint since it indicates the spread between foreign received price and domestic selling price. The effective tariff includes information on input tariff rates, which affect the spread between domestic prices and costs given the relation of output tariffs and output prices. Because a quota may alter the constraint of imports on domestic pricing, a quota dummy variable is included in the analysis.

The nominal tariff rate utilized is an import-weighted measure, defined as collected duties divided by imports. It understates the relevant nominal rate to the extent that higher tariffs reduce imports across goods produced in each industry. The relevant nominal rate should be calculated on a production-weighted basis, indicating the constraint placed on the pricing of domestically produced goods. The complexity of the U.S. tariff code precludes any attempt to calculate this measure.[41]

The effective tariff rate is from Baldwin.[42] It includes some non-tariff barriers to import. Unfortunately, the concordance between Baldwin's industries and the IRS industries is poor, but no more acceptable source of data on effective tariff rates could be found.

A dummy variable indicates those industries whose imports were affected by quotas, whether imposed by the United States or "voluntarily" by foreign governments, during this period. The two most affected industries, sugar (IRS 2060) and petroleum (IRS 2910), are dropped entirely from the sample. Industries receiving a quota dummy value of one are all textile and apparel industries (IRS 2228, 2250, 2298, 2310, 2330, 2380, and 2398) and dairy products (IRS 2020).[43]

RESULTS: DOMESTIC VARIABLES

Results of estimating the noninteractive model are presented as equations 1 and 4 of Tables 2-1 and 2-2. Results of estimating the interactive model using C4 as the interaction variable are presented as equations 2 and 5 of these tables. Results of estimating the interactive model using $1/[1 - \log(C4)]$ as the interaction variable are presented as equations 3 and 6 of these tables. The adjusted explanatory power of the equations is acceptable for cross-sectional analysis. The explanatory power of the interactive specifications is superior to that of noninteractive specifications.

The coefficient on the capital-sales variable indicates that the after-tax opportunity interest cost of capital lies in the range of 2.4 to 3.9 percent. This return appears low, since the highest rated corporate bonds during this period were sold with yields of 5.5 to 8.0 percent.[44]

The growth variable, introduced to capture effects of long-run disequilibrium, has the expected positive coefficient and is significant. Faster growing industries are more profitable.

The effects of both technological and advertising entry barriers are evident. One or both of the scale economy variables, MES/Market and Capital Requirements, are significant. With one insignificant exception they have the hypothesized positive relation. The theoretically preferred cost-adjusted measures are usually more significant than nonadjusted counterparts. The explanatory power of the entire equation increases when the cost-adjusted measures are utilized.

Table 2-1.   Profitability Ordinary Least-Squares Regressions

Equation	1	2	3	4	5	6
Capital/Sales	0.024 (2.58)	0.027 (3.22)	0.025 (3.23)	0.031 (3.35)	0.029 (4.02)	0.033 (4.67)
MES/Market	0.034 (2.18)	-0.013 (0.17)	0.064 (1.60)	—	—	—
Capital Requirements	0.408E-5 (2.02)	0.571E-5 (1.60)	0.549E-5 (1.98)	—	—	—
Cost-adjusted MES/Market	—	—	—	0.041 (2.71)	0.225 (2.23)	0.111 (2.71)
Cost-adjusted Capital Requirements	—	—	—	0.487E-5 (1.88)	0.378E-5 (1.07)	0.629E-5 (2.14)
Advertising Intensity	0.382 (4.76)	1.193 (4.30)	0.841 (4.91)	0.384 (4.90)	1.126 (4.30)	0.828 (5.10)
Growth	0.030 (2.67)	0.069 (2.16)	0.058 (2.58)	0.028 (2.58)	0.044 (1.42)	0.052 (2.42)
C4 (3-digit)	0.026 (2.25)	*	*	0.027 (2.33)	*	*
Scientists & Engineers Fraction	-0.170 (2.31)	-0.327 (1.63)	-0.272 (1.93)	-0.129 (1.85)	-0.266 (1.42)	-0.223 (1.71)
Import Share	-0.033 (0.89)	-0.193 (2.55)	-0.091 (1.47)	-0.048 (1.33)	-0.209 (2.83)	-0.125 (2.07)
Export Share	0.095 (2.33)	0.145 (1.19)	0.167 (2.02)	0.100 (2.54)	0.263 (2.56)	0.204 (2.75)

Nominal Tariff Rate	0.037 (1.61)	0.059 (0.86)	0.073 (1.54)	0.048 (2.10)	0.100 (1.51)	0.109 (2.35)
Constant	0.810E-3 (0.11)	0.015 (2.44)	0.962E-2 (1.60)	-0.525E-2 (0.72)	0.013 (2.37)	0.325E-2 (0.59)
$\bar{R}^2$	0.571	0.617	0.629	0.589	0.656	0.664

Dependent variable: Profit/Sales.

*These equations are interactive in C4 (3-digit). In equations 2 and 5, each variable except Capital/Sales and the Constant is multiplied by C4 (3-digit) prior to regression. In equations 3 and 6, each variable except Capital/Sales and the Constant is multiplied by $\{1/[1 - \log$ C4 (3-digit)]$\}$ prior to regression. The mean of C4 (3-digit) is 0.283. The value of the latter interactive variable at this mean is 0.441.

Number of observations: 71.

t-statistics shown in parentheses. Significance levels for a one-tailed $t(60)$ are:

0.10 : 1.30
0.05 : 1.67
0.01 : 2.39

Table 2-2.   Profitability Ordinary Least-Squares Regressions

Equation	1	2	3	4	5	6
Capital/Sales	0.031 (3.38)	0.028 (3.61)	0.030 (3.89)	0.039 (4.20)	0.035 (4.86)	0.038 (5.28)
MES/Market	0.026 (1.51)	0.033 (1.82)	0.035 (1.99)	—	—	—
Capital Requirements	0.581E-5 (2.93)	0.645E-5 (2.76)	0.656E-5 (2.95)	—	—	—
Cost-adjusted MES/Market	—	—	—	0.031 (1.84)	0.040 (2.35)	0.042 (2.50)
Cost-adjusted Capital Requirements	—	—	—	0.745E-5 (3.13)	0.941E-5 (3.50)	0.943E-5 (3.61)
Advertising Intensity	0.377 (4.23)	0.465 (4.14)	0.485 (4.59)	0.378 (4.33)	0.454 (4.25)	0.480 (4.77)
Growth	0.027 (2.29)	0.053 (2.83)	0.046 (2.76)	0.026 (2.24)	0.048 (2.70)	0.043 (2.69)
C4 (4-digit)	0.011 (0.71)	*	*	0.014 (0.91)	*	*
Scientists & Engineers Fraction	-0.179 (2.24)	-0.352 (3.18)	-0.300 (2.91)	-0.126 (1.62)	-0.265 (2.62)	-0.219 (2.33)
Import Share	-0.017 (0.42)	-0.011 (0.17)	-0.014 (0.23)	-0.034 (0.85)	-0.056 (0.84)	-0.051 (0.89)
Export Share	0.087 (2.05)	0.134 (1.98)	0.130 (2.12)	0.096 (2.35)	0.159 (2.55)	0.150 (2.63)

Nominal Tariff Rate	0.040	0.102	0.084	0.055	0.133	0.112
	(1.68)	(2.30)	(2.17)	(2.33)	(3.10)	(3.00)
Constant	-0.422E-2	0.610E-2	0.277E-2	-0.012	0.822E-4	-0.413E-2
	(0.44)	(0.99)	(0.42)	(1.43)	(0.01)	(0.67)
$\bar{R}^2$	0.539	0.601	0.593	0.557	0.639	0.629

Dependent variable: Profit/Sales.

*These equations are interactive in C4 (4-digit). In equations 2 and 5, each variable except Capital/Sales and the Constant is multiplied by C4 (4-digit) prior to regression. In equations 3 and 6, each variable except Capital/Sales and the Constant is multiplied by {1/[1 — log C4 (4-digit)]} prior to regression. The mean of C4 (4-digit) is 0.553. The value of the latter interactive variable at this mean is 0.628.

Number of observations: 71.

t-statistics shown in parentheses. Significance levels for a one-tailed $t(60)$ are:

    0.10 : 1.30
    0.05 : 1.67
    0.01 : 2.39

Advertising is shown as a particularly significant barrier to entry. The results indicate that an advertising expense of $0.10 per $1.00 of sales tends to increase price by $0.04 or more in addition to the recovery of the $0.10 cost. Some of this excess return is justified by the riskiness of advertising investment, especially the initial spending to establish a brand name or corporate image.[45] But it is doubtful that this return reflects only risk adjustment; rather, much of it probably represents monopoly profit based on the product differentiation-advertising entry barrier.

Research and development activity receives no support as an entry barrier as indicated by the negative coefficient on scientists and engineers as a fraction of employment. Expensing of R & D activities, rather than capitalization of their investment value, could produce this result.

Concentration is significant only when measured directly at the 3-digit level of analysis in the noninteractive regressions. Its importance is better indicated by the increase in explanatory power (R^2) of the interactive regressions, equations 2, 3, 5, and 6, over comparably specified noninteractive regressions, equations 1 and 4. The hypothesis that concentration reflects the state of domestic producer competition receives strong support. Concentration measured directly at the 3-digit level appears superior in explanatory power to the weighted average 4-digit concentration ratio.[46]

The statistical importance of the noninteractive and interactive variables is tested in regressions including both sets of variables. Results of these tests are reported in Table 2-3. The regression results are based on estimation of Equation 2-19, not including the quota dummy or FDI intensity. The regression results are not reported because multicollinearity renders the coefficients uninterpretable.

The test results reject the null hypothesis that the interactive variables add no explanatory power in six of the equations at the 0.01 level and in one at the 0.10 level. The test fails to reject this null hypothesis once. The tests fail to reject the null hypothesis that the noninteractive variables add no significant explanatory power in the C4 (4-digit) equations. The statistical importance of the interactive variables is more robust, but both sets of variables may be statistically important. These tests strongly support the hypothesis that barriers and concentration are interactive in their effect on pricing and profitability.

In short, with the exception of R & D intensity, support for the effect of domestic entry barriers on product pricing and profitability is strong. These results replicate a number of other studies.[47] In addition, the interactive results greatly expand the empirical support for considering barriers and producer competition, represented by producer concentration, as jointly determining long-run prices and profits. This interaction has previously been explored only in relatively less complex empirical models.[48]

RESULTS: INTERNATIONAL VARIABLES

Tables 2-1 and 2-2 also present results of inclusion of international trade variables in the determination of profitability. Before examining

Table 2-3. Hypothesis Testing

This table presents results of testing the joint significance of noninteractive or interactive variables in unreported regressions. The null hypothesis is that one set of variables, either the noninteractive or interactive variables, adds no significant explanatory power to a regression containing both sets of variables, Capital/Sales, and a constant term. The specifications of these tested equations are thus the equations 2, 3, 5, and 6 of Tables 2-1 and 2-2, to which the noninteractive variables MES/Market, Capital Requirements, Advertising Intensity, Growth, Scientists & Engineers Fraction, Import Share, Export Share, and Nominal Tariff Rate have been added.

F-statistics	C4 (3-digit)		C4 (4-digit)	
MES/Market and Capital Requirements	*Unadjusted*	*Cost-adjusted*	*Unadjusted*	*Cost-adjusted*
Noninteractive variables add no explanatory power to variables interactive in C4	4.25	2.75	0.67	1.35
Noninteractive variables add no explanatory power to variables interactive in $[1/(1 - \log C4)]$	3.90	2.53	0.92	1.76
Variables interactive in C4 add no explanatory power to noninteractive variables	6.35	5.38	1.75	3.13
Variables interactive in $[1/(1 - \log C4)]$ add no explanatory power to noninteractive variables	6.35	5.38	1.85	3.36

Degrees of freedom are (8, 53).

Significance levels for $F(8, 60)$ are:

0.10 : 1.77
0.05 : 2.10
0.01 : 2.82

these results individually, we test the joint significance of the three international trade variables.

Results of testing the joint influence of import share, export share, and the nominal tariff in the equations of Tables 2-1 and 2-2 are presented in Table 2-4. In the theoretically preferred equations 5 and 6, which are interactive and use cost-adjusted technological barrier measures, the null hypothesis is rejected at the 0.01 level. In the noninteractive equation 4, which also has cost-adjusted technological variables, the null hypothesis is rejected at the 0.05 level. The null hypothesis is not rejected at the 0.10 level in only one of the other equations, all of which use unadjusted technological variables. Even for the United States, often considered a relatively closed economy, international influences are significant in the determination of prices and profits.

The coefficient on the import share is always negative, but it is significant only in equations 2, 3, 5, and 6 of Table 2-1, the interactive 3-digit concentration equations. Actual import penetration reflects the constraint placed by imports on domestic pricing. This constraint is more severe in relatively concentrated domestic industries. This result, however, is not robust to the choice of concentration measure.

The nominal tariff rate is positively and significantly related to price-cost margins. Tariff protection is utilized by domestic industry to raise price over cost while avoiding severe import competition. The degree of utilization is a positive function of the degree to which

Table 2-4. Hypothesis Testing

This table presents results of testing the joint significance of the international trade variables in the equations of Tables 2-1 and 2-2. The null hypothesis is that the variables Import Share, Export Share, and Nominal Tariff Rate add no explanatory power to the equations shown in Tables 2-1 and 2-2.

F-statistics	Table 2-1	Table 2-2
Equation 1	2.33	2.02
2	2.72	2.77
3	2.31	2.68
4	3.20	3.11
5	4.39	4.89
6	4.25	4.68

Degrees of freedom for equations 1 and 4 are (3, 60). Degrees of freedom for equations 2, 3, 5, and 6 are (3, 61).

Significance levels for $F(3, 60)$ are:

$$0.10 : 2.18$$
$$0.05 : 2.76$$
$$0.01 : 4.13$$

domestic producer competition is circumscribed although this conclusion is strongly supported only by the interactive C4 (4-digit) results.

The coefficient of the nominal tariff is small and indicates that even for the most highly concentrated industries only 10 percent to 13 percent of the tariff is reflected in increased after-tax profitability. Price increases relative to cost could reflect up to 25 percent of the tariff although part of the extra profit will be taxed away by the federal corporate income tax. Additional price increases relative to cost due indirectly to the tariff through its lowering of the actual import share are also possible. Nonetheless, the results indicate that domestic prices are not raised by the full amount of the tariff unless domestic costs also increase substantially. Alternatively, perhaps import prices do not rise by the full amount of the tariff. If import prices do not rise, domestic producers cannot increase price by the full tariff. Foreign firms may absorb part of the tariff.

Export share is significantly and positively related to price-cost margins. This result is not likely due to high collinearity with the scientists and engineers fraction. In equations omitting the international variables, the coefficient on the scientists and engineers fraction is always negative and often significant. There is no support statistically for a domestic R & D entry barrier.

Rather, this result indicates that export profitability is greater than domestic profitability. Domestic pricing is determined by domestic entry barriers and the state of domestic producer competition. Apparently, export pricing is less constrained than domestic pricing. In export markets the large U.S. exporters may face neither the competition of their smaller domestic rivals nor sufficient foreign competition to force competitive pricing of exports.

The export ability of U.S. industries is directly related to intensive use of skilled labor, including R & D personnel. In the United States entry barriers are relatively low in these industries if skilled labor is sufficiently mobile among firms, other things being equal. Casual evidence supports relatively high mobility of R & D personnel in the United States.[49] The domestic maket is competitive as small firms enter and exit easily. These small firms often lack the resources to export so the large U.S. firms face less competition from smaller U.S. firms in export markets.

Access to skilled labor may be a more formidable entry barrier in foreign markets.[50] Not only is the supply of skilled labor relatively smaller than in the United States, but interfirm mobility is also lower. Again, evidence about foreign R & D personnel supports these hypotheses.[51] Thus U.S. firms face less competition in export markets and exploit their oligopolistic advantage.

The opportunity to export enhances profitability in that U.S. exporters charge higher prices on export sales than on domestic sales. Exporting may also allow R & D expenses and other relatively fixed costs to be spread over a larger volume, thereby reducing unit cost. Exporting enhances the profitability of U.S. firms without any special effect on domestic prices.

Results of estimation of equations including the quota dummy, the effective tariff rate in place of the nominal tariff rate, or FDI intensity are not presented. These variables are always insignificant if added to the equations of Tables 2-1 and 2-2. The insignificance of the quota dummy may be indicative of the political economy of quota imposition. Only those industries severely disrupted, apparently by import competition, receive quota relief, and this relief only allows them to earn a barely normal rate of return. Of course sugar and petroleum are omitted from the sample. The insignificance of the effective tariff rate may be due to the poor concordance between Baldwin's industries and the IRS industries.[52]

An attempt to test Bergsten, Horst, and Moran's feedback hypothesis of foreign direct investment on profitability indicates FDI is not significant although data limitations bias the results in this direction.[53] It is possible that their significant results in favor of the feedback hypothesis are the product of their inclusion of very small firms and their omission of export and import variables. Small firms tend to have low reported profits and little FDI. Because of correlations among import share, export share, and FDI intensity, their results using only FDI intensity may reflect not only its own, apparently small, feedback effect, but also part of the effect of import competition and export opportunity demonstrated above.

International influences, especially import competition, export ability, and U.S. tariff rates, are significant influences on domestic pricing and profits. Previous investigators who treated the United States as a closed economy have failed to identify and incorporate into their analyses one set of important factors in the market structure-conduct-performance nexus.

CONCLUSIONS

This chapter discussed the barriers to entry model of long-run industrial market equilibrium, expanding it to include foreign trade influences. Empirical results presented support the model in demonstrating the interaction of entry barriers, producer competition, and international trade influences on the determination of the long-run equilibrium relation between price and cost.

The theory and results are based on microeconomic, partial equilibrium models of industrial markets. To analyze the welfare implications, especially of tariffs and quotas, general equilibrium considerations are also important. While no significant relationship between quotas and price-cost margins was found, quotas likely impede reallocation of resources used in production domestically. Quotas inhibit exit from industries that have a comparative cost disadvantage in the United States and thus reduce the productive efficiency of the U.S. economy. Tariffs produce this same allocative inefficiency and allow firms, especially firms in relatively concentrated industries, to raise domestic price over cost.

The assumption of cost minimization made at the beginning of this chapter may be questioned. In highly competitive industries, competitive pressure likely enforces cost minimization. However, less competitive industries generate less pressure to minimize costs as firms more easily realize a comfortable rate of return on investment. Therefore, the empirical results indicating that less competitive industries earn excess profits may only unmask a part of their inefficiency. Technical inefficiency and excessive cost may also be present. Measures of technical efficiency could not be constructed.

The analysis presented above demonstrates allocative inefficiency due to market power. Two major policy implications are derived from these results. First, antitrust action aimed at reducing producer concentration may be effective in improving allocative efficiency even if the underlying barriers cannot be modified. Second, U.S. commercial policy toward imports is an additional instrument to affect domestic pricing. Imports restrict domestic pricing in relatively concentrated industries, but tariffs, quotas, and other nontariff barriers reduce this constraint. Thus free trade, which allows a maximum amount of foreign competition, should be adopted for domestically concentrated industries to lessen market power and restrain domestic pricing in these industries. Policy implications are explored further in Chapter 5.

NOTES

1. J.S. Bain, *Barriers to New Competition*, 1956, finds that in his sample of industries at least 70 percent of output was produced in plants of minimum efficient scale. In addition, the "fringe" may often economically be justified as minimizing the sum of transport and production costs.

2. Literature on the managerially controlled firm suggests this need not be true. See K.J. Cohen and R.M. Cyert, *Theory of the Firm*, 1965, or O.E. Williamson, "Managerial Discretion and Business Behavior," *American Economic Review*, December 1963.

3. See H.C. Eastman and S. Stykolt, *The Tariff and Competition in Canada*, 1967, or H. Bloch, "Prices, Costs and Profits in Canadian Manufacturing: The Influence of Tariffs and Concentration," *Canadian Journal of Economics*, November 1974.

4. G.J. Hurdle, "Leverage, Risk, Market Structure, and Profitability," *Review of Economics and Statistics*, November 1974, attempts to explore risk empirically.

5. Hurdle concludes that risk does not supersede other influences discussed subsequently in this chapter. R.J. Stonebraker, "Corporate Profits and Risk of Entry," *Review of Economics and Statistics*, February 1976, concludes that the risk of large firms does not explain the interindustry variation in their rates of return. Rather, small firm risk, which he concludes is caused by entry barriers, explains statistically the variation in large firms' rates of return.

6. J.S. Bain.

7. For an introduction, see R.E. Caves, *American Industry: Structure, Conduct, Performance*, fourth edition, 1977.

8. J.S. Bain, "Theory Concerning the Condition of Entry," in J.S. Bain, *Essays on Price Theory and Industrial Organization*, 1972.

9. J.S. Bain, "Theory Concerning the Condition of Entry."

10. J.S. Bain, *Barriers to New Competition*, ch. 5.

11. W.S. Comanor and T.A. Wilson, *Advertising and Market Power*, 1974, ch. 4.

12. W.S. Comanor and T.A. Wilson.

13. Concentration is determined at least partly by domestic entry barriers. See Chapter 4.

14. For instance, see W.S. Comanor and T.A. Wilson, ch. 6, or M.E. Porter, "Consumer Behavior, Retailer Power and Market Performance in Consumer Goods Industries," *Review of Economics and Statistics*, November 1974.

15. L. Esposito and F.E. Esposito, "Foreign Competition and Domestic Industry Profitability," *Review of Economics and Statistics*, November 1971, and E. Pagoulatos and R. Sorenson, "International Trade, International Investment, and Industrial Profitability of U.S. Manufacturing," *Southern Economic Journal*, January 1976.

16. Of course, if c is greater than p_M, there will be no domestic production.

17. If increments to world supply are made by new firms, they need not be able to overcome these barriers so easily.

18. Focal points are important in games theory approaches to oligopolistic behavior. F.M. Scherer, *Industrial Market Structure and Economic Performance*, 1970, pp. 179-182.

19. R.E. Caves, *International Trade, International Investment, and Imperfect Markets*, 1974, pp. 1-4.

20. D.C. Mueller and J.E. Tilton, "Research and Development Costs as a Barrier to Entry," *Canadian Journal of Economics*, November 1969.

21. F.M. Scherer, pp. 357-362.

22. Exemption of collective export associations is provided in the Webb-Pomerene Act. U.S. Department of Justice, Antitrust Division, *Antitrust Guide for International Operations*, January 1977, pp. 2-4.

23. C.F. Bergsten, T. Horst, and T. Moran, *American Multinationals and American Interests*, 1978, partially summarized in T. Horst, "American Multinationals and the U.S. Economy," *American Economic Review*, May 1976.

24. Strictly, we would prefer $\delta(\text{Profit/Sales})/\delta C4 \geq 0$ always. This condition is only true if $\Sigma b_i X_i \geq 0$. All X_i except growth and the effective tariff rate must be non-negative by definition. Only the effective tariff rate is negative in the sample. All b_i except that on the import share are expected positive.

25. Both B.T. Gale, "Market Share and Rate of Return," *Review of Economics and Statistics*, November 1972, and M.E. Porter discuss and test a growth-concentration interaction. They expect and find that each of growth and concentration is positively related to profitability, but that the interactive term is negatively related. Although this hypothesis is not directly tested here, no clear pattern of signs on the noninteractive and interactive coefficients on growth is found in estimation of Equation 2-19. At least one of the signs is always positive.

26. P.D. Qualls, "Concentration, Barriers to Entry and Long Run Economic Profit Margins," *Journal of Industrial Economics*, April 1972, discusses this point.

27. L.W. Weiss, "Optimal Plant Size and the Extent of Suboptimal Capacity," in Masson and Qualls, eds., *Essays on Industrial Organization in Honor of Joe S. Bain*, 1976.

28. L.W. Weiss, "The Geographic Size of Markets in Manufacturing," *Review of Economics and Statistics*, August 1972.

29. J.S. Bain, "Theory Concerning the Condition of Entry."

30. R.E. Caves, J. Khalizadeh-Shirazi, and M.E. Porter, "Scale Economies in Statistical Analyses of Market Power," *Review of Economics and Statistics*, May 1975.

31. The variable is a poor measure of total factor productivity across plant size to the extent that it reflects physical capital variations, labor skill variations, market power differences, and product mix variations across plant size instead of productivity.

32. The Herfindahl index is defined as the sum of squares of each firm's share of industry shipments. The entropy measure is represented as E in

$$\frac{1}{E} = \prod_i (\frac{1}{s_i})^{s_i}$$

where s_i is the ith firm's share of industry shipments.

33. R.L. Nelson, *Concentration in the Manufacturing Industries of the United States*, 1963, and R.W. Kilpatrick, "The Choice Among Alternative Measures of Industrial Concentration," *Review of Economics and Statistics*, May 1967.

34. W.G. Shepherd, *Market Power and Economic Welfare*, 1970.

35. L.W. Weiss, "The Geographic Size of Markets in Manufacturing." The Weiss method may be biased toward low estimates of radius shipped and number of markets. Goods that are easily transportable may not be shipped

long distances if the locational pattern of production is rationalized and sales are made only to proximate buyers. Weiss notes this effect only in industries that face centralized locational demand. If these goods are easily transportable, he treats these industries as if they were a national market. We follow his convention here. In adjusting Shepherd's concentration ratios, only four relatively small 4-digit SIC industries were considered national by Shepherd but measured as regional by Weiss. The Weiss method established that ten 4-digit industries considered by Shepherd to be regional were national on the basis of distance shipped. Thus for the vast majority of 4-digit industries, Weiss and Shepherd reach similar conclusions about geographical extent of market. There is more serious disagreement between Weiss and Schwartzman and Bodoff. Of Schwartzman and Bodoff's fifty-one 4-digit regional industries, Weiss establishes that nineteen are national on the basis of distance shipped and assumes that five others are local. Of Schwartzman and Bodoff's eleven local industries, Weiss establishes that three are regional on the basis of distance shipped. D. Schwartzman and J. Bodoff, "Concentration in Regional and Local Industries," *Southern Economic Journal*, January 1971.

36. Statistics are reported by asset size class with the number of firms in each size class also reported. Where the smallest size class needed to identify the four largest firms actually raised the total number of firms above four (e.g., the largest size class has three firms and the next largest size class has two firms), each firm in this size class was assumed to be of the same size. This results in probable underestimation of concentration for these industries.

37. R.W. Kilpatrick, "The Validity of the Average Concentration Ratio as a Measure of Industry Structure," *Southern Economic Journal*, April 1976.

38. R.W. Kilpatrick, "The Validity of the Average Concentration Ratio as a Measure of Industry Structure."

39. W. Gruber, D. Mehta, and R. Vernon, "The R & D Factor in International Trade and International Investment of United States Industries," *Journal of Political Economy*, February 1967.

40. National Science Foundation, *Industrial R & D Funds in Relation to Other Economic Variables*, NSF 64-25, 1964.

41. U.S. Bureau of the Census, *Schedule A: Rates of Duty and Tariff Paragraphs*.

42. R.E. Baldwin, *Nontariff Distortions of International Trade*, 1970.

43. I. Mintz, *U.S. Import Quotas: Costs and Consequences*, 1973.

44. *Economic Report of the President*, 1977, Table B-63.

45. Investment aspects of advertising are explored by L.W. Weiss, "Advertising, Profits, and Corporate Taxes," *Review of Economics and Statistics*, November 1969.

46. For a discussion of the relative merits of the two concentration measures, see S.E. Boyle, "The Average Concentration Ratio: An Inappropriate Measure of Industry Structure," *Journal of Political Economy*, March-April 1973; J.J. Siegfried, "In Defense of the Average Concentration Ratio," *Journal of Political Economy*, December 1975; and R.W. Kilpatrick, "The Validity of the Average Concentration Ratio as a Measure of Industry Structure."

47. For instance, see W.S. Comanor and T.A. Wilson, ch. 6, or M.E. Porter.

48. J.S. Bain, *Barriers to New Competition*; H.M. Mann, "Seller Concentration, Barriers to Entry, and Rates of Return in Thirty Industries, 1950-1960,"*Review of Economics and Statistics*, August 1966; and P.D. Qualls, "Stability and Persistence of Economic Profit Margins in Highly Concentrated Industries," *Southern Economic Journal*, April 1974.

49. Mobility is high in the semiconductor industry. D.W. Webbink, *The Semiconductor Industry: A Survey of Structure, Conduct, Performance*, 1977, pp. 101-103.

50. Barriers to the entry of small domestic firms outside of the United States are high in the semiconductor industry. J.E. Tilton, *International Diffusion of Technology: The Case of Semiconductors*, 1971.

51. Organization for Economic Cooperation and Development, *Gaps in Technology: Electronic Components*, 1968.

52. R.E. Baldwin.

53. Their data suffer from even more severe biases of the same kind described here because they omit all identifiable foreign profit from their measure of industry profit.

❊   *Chapter 3*

International Trade Patterns

The previous chapter analyzed the effects of international trade and domestic market structure on the profitability of U.S. firms. Domestic market structure and conduct also affect international trade patterns.

This chapter analyzes influences on the commodity composition of U.S. trade in manufactures. Theories of comparative advantage, both Heckscher-Ohlin and product life cycle, are discussed, additional influences such as tariffs, transport costs, and product differentiation are considered, and the effects of U.S. market structure and conduct on trade are analyzed. Empirical specifications are developed and applied to data on trade in manufactures at the 3-digit level of industry definition. A full literature survey is not attempted here as Stern[1] and Morrall[2] have presented surveys recently.

Statistical analysis of the net trade positions, export shares, and import shares across industries indicate that the Heckscher-Ohlin theories of comparative advantage and the product life cycle theory are complementary. Both are important in explaining trade patterns. Transportability and governmentally imposed divergences from free trade are additional influences. Among aspects of market structure and conduct, advertising and its related required investment in promotion and marketing of highly advertised goods act as a barrier to trade. Foreign firms tend to avoid these investments because of their risk and because foreign firms may lack knowledge of the domestic market.

HECKSCHER-OHLIN THEORIES OF
COMPARATIVE ADVANTAGE

The initial formulation of the Heckscher-Ohlin theory of trade, which states that a country exports goods that utilize relatively intensively the factor inputs found relatively abundantly in the country, was based upon a multiple factor analysis of production.[3] As the theory was formalized mathematically, the number of factors considered was reduced to two, usually capital and labor. However, when Leontief tested the pattern of trade implications of this theory, he found that the United States, certainly a capital-abundant country, exported goods that were more labor-intensive on average than her import substitutes.[4] Suggestions for the cause of these findings were plentiful. Some suggestions, such as factor-intensity reversals in production or differing technology across countries, negated the theory. Others required only modification of the theory, such modifications as the impact of U.S. tariffs, the importance of natural resources, which can be considered additional (and often industry-specific) factors of production, and the improper treatment of labor as a single, homogeneous factor of production. Here the delineation of the relevant factors of production is discussed. The next section presents the product life cycle approach to international trade, a rival of Heckscher-Ohlin theories.

The major refinement of Heckscher-Ohlin factors of production is the treatment of labor. Leontief measured labor in man-years, assuming it homogeneous. However, labor is not homogeneous, as implied by the distinction of skilled from unskilled workers or more generally in considering each worker to possess a certain amount of human capital. Different products require different mixes of various skill classes of labor in production. Therefore, the pattern of trade in manufactures may be determined by each country's total available mix of different skill classes of workers. Reinforcing this hypothesis is the observation that capital is increasingly mobile across national boundaries, both in the form of portfolio investment and foreign direct investment, while labor remains a relatively immobile factor. The United States is relatively abundant in skilled labor and according to the Heckscher-Ohlin theory should export goods that are relatively intensive in skilled labor.[5]

Natural resources are important for certain aspects of U.S. trade. Trade in agricultural commodities is dependent on climate and land. The United States has a relative advantage in the production of most temperate foodstuffs. A relative disadvantage is probable in tropical foodstuffs. Factor-intensity reversals in the production of some agricultural commodities are also possible.[6] Because these resource factors are difficult to quantify and because trade in foodstuffs is often severely distorted by domestic agricultural policies, agricultural trade is not considered further.

The United States is losing comparative advantage in mineral resources. At present, the United States is a large net importer of most mineral commodities such as metallic ores.[7] Natural resource disadvantage may cause part of the Leontief paradox as extraction of these minerals is relatively capital-intensive. This study also does not further consider mineral trade.

However, we must evaluate the effect of the availability of natural resources on trade in manufactures. Raw material availability potentially affects the food, tobacco, wood products and paper, petroleum, and basic metals sectors. Transport and tariff considerations, as well as relative factor endowments, are likely to influence the location of production. Thus bauxite mined outside of the United States may be processed into alumina at the point of mining or shipped raw to the United States for processing.[8] The location of refining may not respond in the same way to comparative advantage as the location of more "foot-loose" industries such as machinery or clothing.

Thus, the Heckscher-Ohlin theory, extended to include natural resource considerations and to differentiate qualities of labor, could explain the U.S. pattern of trade in manufactures. Empirical tests are presented later in this chapter. Next we consider an alternative theory of this pattern, the product life cycle theory.

THE PRODUCT LIFE CYCLE THEORY
OF COMPARATIVE ADVANTAGE

Since World War II the United States has steadily increased research and development activities and the introduction of new manufactured products. This observation served as the basis for the formalization of an alternative theory of comparative advantage based upon the product life cycle.[9] Its originators presented the theory as a scenario based on the life cycle of a single product. The theory may pertain especially to the United States.

Development and introduction of new products is based upon perceived potential demand. The United States, with its high per capita income and relative labor scarcity, offers a large potential market for the relatively sophisticated, often time- and labor-saving new consumer and capital goods. Initial production of a new product is located close to the intended major market because efficient monitoring of consumer response is necessary. This production is labor-intensive relative to capital as production runs are small and the production process and the product are unstandardized. The need for flexibility in adapting and refining the new product and its production processes leads to relatively skilled-labor-intensive production. Demand in other countries is satisfied by U.S. export. This phase of the product life cycle, introduction and growth, is considered the height of U.S. comparative advantage.

As acceptance in the United States and world economic growth expand the market for the product, production increases, leading to longer production runs. The product becomes standardized, and its production processes are refined and standardized as the need for flexibility diminishes. The production processes are now more capital-intensive relative to labor and less skilled-labor-intensive.

The search for low-cost locations leads to production abroad. The threat of foreclosure of foreign markets may speed the process as U.S. firms engage in defensive foreign investment. Comparative advantage shifts away from the United States, and the United States becomes a net importer of this good.

A few implications of this product life cycle approach are evident. First, it explains Leontief's paradoxical cross-section results. The U.S. exports newer, relatively unstandardized, relatively (skilled) labor-intensive products. Second, although the theory is discussed as an alternative to Heckscher-Ohlin theories of trade, it is best considered complementary to the Heckscher-Ohlin theories. While demand considerations are stressed more than in Heckscher-Ohlin theory, the basis for U.S. comparative advantage is also the relative abundance of factors, especially labor trained as scientists and engineers, needed to undertake research and development activities. With maturity the location of production shifts out of the United States due to U.S. comparative disadvantage in less skilled labor. Relatively mobile capital internationally aids this process.

Thus, while treatment of these theories as competing may be fruitful in statistical analysis, their complementarity must also be considered. Next several additional factors affecting international trade are discussed.

GOVERNMENT POLICY AND
PRODUCT CHARACTERISTICS

Two theories of the U.S. international trade pattern have been discussed. A number of additional influences on this pattern exist. This section discusses government restrictions on trade, in the form of tariffs, quotas, and other nontariff barriers (NTBs) to trade, and two influences not usually considered explicitly at the theoretical level, transportability and product differentiation. These latter influences are used to introduce the theory of intraindustry trade.

Tariffs increase the differential between U.S. price of an imported good and its foreign net price. They diminish the importance of comparative advantage in dictating trade patterns by lessening the incentive to export and may actually eliminate trade based on comparative advantage.[10] Their distorting influence should be considered in any analysis of the determinants of trade. However, a number of issues relate to the use of tariffs in this analysis.

Consumers in the United States base consumption decisions on the prices of foreign goods and their domestically produced substitutes. Therefore the nominal U.S. tariff affects U.S. consumer choice because the tariff tends to raise the price of foreign goods. However, domestic producers have more complex considerations. Tariffs on imported goods that compete with their final product improve their domestic competitive position, but tariffs on material inputs tend to weaken their competitive position. The effective rate of protection, defined as

$$e_i = (t_i - \sum_j a_{ij} t_j) / (1 - \sum_j a_{ij}) \qquad (3\text{-}1)$$

where e_i is the effective rate of protection, ts are nominal tariff rates, and a_{ij} is the share of each intermediate input j in one dollar's worth of output of good i at world prices, measures the incentive to increase domestic production of import substitutes. Both the nominal and the effective rates are therefore important in affecting the volume of imports. U.S. exports are affected in similar ways by foreign tariffs as well as being affected by U.S. tariffs on their material inputs.[11]

Quotas affect trade flows more directly by setting a maximum amount (expressed in value or volume terms) of imports. The United States in the late 1960s had quotas on sugar, textiles and apparel, dairy products, meat, petroleum, steel, and numerous other products, although some of these quotas were disguised as "voluntary" export quotas nominally set by foreign countries.[12] For these years Mintz concluded the quotas on sugar, dairy products, and petroleum were important in restricting imports and raising U.S. prices, whereas the quotas on textiles and apparel (covering only cotton before 1971), meat, and steel were relatively less important. No analysis is here attempted of foreign quota effects on U.S. exports, although this analysis would be especially important if agricultural products were investigated.

Governments impose a wide variety of other restrictions on international trade, ranging from Buy American regulations to standards of weights and measures, which together with quotas are termed non-tariff barriers to trade.[13] Their influence is difficult to analyze because of their variety and because of the difficulty in modeling their quantitative impact.

Besides governmental action, a number of other influences may affect international trade patterns. Natural characteristics of the product relating to weight, bulk, fragility, and perishability affect the flow of goods across international borders in the same way as they affect the flow of goods between geographical regions within a country. As transport costs per unit shipped increase, the differential between the domestic price of the imported good and the price received by the foreign producer increases. Increasing costliness of transportation tends to decrease international trade by affecting the incentive to export.

Product differentiation may also influence trade patterns. Basic Heckscher-Ohlin theory assumes products to be homogeneous and therefore focuses on differences in production costs across countries. The product life cycle theory is based upon dynamic product differentiation. Goods that are intrinsically differentiable lend themselves to research and development of new variations.

Most manufactured goods can be considered to reflect varying degrees of nonhomogeneity. For consumer goods physical differences, branding, advertising, and differences in perceptions all contribute to differentiation of products within an industry (defined to include close but not necessarily perfect substitutes). For producer goods delivery dates, servicing, and the ability to customize differentiate firms within an industry. Thus, the ability to achieve, maintain, and communicate product differentiation may be an additional basis for comparative advantage among firms located across countries but producing within the same industry.

These latter two influences, transportability and product differentiation, have contributed to the theory of intraindustry trade.[14] Intraindustry trade is the part of an industry's gross trade that is matched by imports and exports, giving the appearance of cross-hauling between countries. Even at very fine levels of industry definition, this trade still appears quantitatively important.

Transportability influences intraindustry trade in two ways. For goods whose difficulty of transport would otherwise preclude international trade, trade between firms located close to the border and proximate foreign buyers may occur. Such trade is especially important when national boundaries do not reflect natural transportation impediments. International trade based on proximity likely leads to intraindustry trade if industry trade is measured at the national level.

Otherwise, ease of transportability allows larger trade volume. Other determinants of the extent of intraindustry trade become important. Intraindustry trade may be based on aspects of product differentiation. Producers from various countries may each fill relatively small foreign market niches left open by domestic producers.

Life cycle aspects of product differentiation may also give rise to intraindustry trade. Within a given industry, the United States exports the newly developed products and imports the relatively older products. Foreign direct investment speeds this process and may contribute directly to intraindustry trade if intermediate goods are sent abroad for foreign processing and then reexported to the United States. The materials exported and the good reimported often are classified in the same industry.

We have identified several theories of U.S. comparative advantage and have discussed several additional influences on the pattern of trade. The final portion of this analysis focuses on the effects of domestic market structure on the pattern of trade.

MARKET STRUCTURE AND CONDUCT

Elements of domestic market structure and conduct were discussed in Chapter 2. They include technological considerations, both minimum efficient scale of plant relative to market size and capital requirements for entry at efficient scale, product differentiation and advertising, domestic producer concentration, and pricing.

For foreign producers considering export to the United States, domestic market structure affects both the incentives to export and the barriers. Incentives depend on the difference between price and cost. Comparative advantage focuses on costs across countries. If domestic price is elevated above domestic producer cost, foreign producers perceive an incentive to export in addition to any comparative cost advantage.

Barriers to entry faced by potential domestic competitors may confront foreign firms considering exporting to the United States. Since these firms are already established, the technological barriers are probably not especially important. Only firms that have achieved minimum efficient scale are in a position to compete in export markets.[15]

Product differentiation and advertising intensity are likely to affect foreign firms. Product differentiation may allow foreign producers to satisfy certain market niches and thus may actually encourage exporting to the United States. However, if the differentiation is based on advertising, foreign firms may forego exporting. The need to develop a promotional campaign and to establish a distribution network discourages trade because these marketing activities require additional and especially risky capital outlays. The foreign firm faces an advertising-product differentiation barrier similar to that faced by potential domestic entrants. The foreign firm may face the additional disadvantage of lacking knowledge of the U.S. market and the best approaches to selling in this market.

The analysis contrasts market structure import barriers and import incentives caused by the elevation of domestic price above cost. Domestic price may be elevated above cost in the presence of barriers to entry facing domestic firms as discussed in the previous chapter. Barriers to import are likely to be a subset of domestic entry barriers. The distinction made here avoids confusion of the two roles of domestic market structure in influencing the commodity pattern of trade[16] and should allow both effects to be isolated by statistical analysis.

Many of the same considerations likely face U.S. firms exporting, and thus advertising and product differentiation could modify the pattern of U.S. exports predicted by comparative advantage. Note that firms in industries that charge prices in excess of economic cost domestically do not necessarily limit exports because price discrimination that allows a lower foreign price may be a profit-maximizing decision. Domestic pricing decisions are independent of export pricing decisions unless reimport or foreign governmental reaction is probable.

NET TRADE: SPECIFICATIONS AND RESULTS

Our method of statistical analysis of the U.S. pattern of trade is a cross-section analysis of direct factor requirements and other characteristics of an industry. In this section analysis of the determinants of the net trade pattern of manufactures is undertaken. The next section explores intraindustry trade, and the following section analyzes export and import patterns separately.

The net trade position of each industry is defined as exports minus imports. For cross-industry analysis, the scale of the variable must be adjusted.[17] Two scaling variables are used here. The first is total trade, exports plus imports. The second is shipments plus imports, a quantity that may be termed available domestic supply.[18] Out of this available supply, both domestic consumption demand and export demand must be satisfied.

The ratio net trade to total trade has often been used because it implicitly controls for transportability. Industries whose products are not easily transportable tend to have less total trade, but their net trade position should still be determined by comparative advantage and other considerations previously discussed. However, this scaling property of the variable may be at least partially undesirable. The ratio may attach too much importance to the small net trade positions of industries in which little international trade occurs. The second ratio, net trade to available supply, controls for industry size but does not control for transportability.[19] Industries that have the larger net trade position relative to industry size are given more importance in the statistical analysis.

Not all of the influences previously discussed can be tested empirically using these dependent variables. Data on certain influences are too costly to obtain. This is especially true of the governmental variables. For instance, U.S. tariffs and quotas can be easily measured, but the tariffs and quotas facing U.S. exporters are more difficult to quantify and summarize. Other influences are expected to have the same qualitative influence on the volume of exports and imports, respectively, and these influences cannot be analyzed in this framework. For instance, advertising has been postulated as a barrier to trade, both for exports and imports.

Use of net trade position is limited to exploring theories of comparative advantage:

$$\text{Net Trade Position} = f_1 \text{ (Capital-Labor Ratio, Labor Skill,}$$

$$\text{Natural Resource Dummy, Scientists \& Engineers Fraction)}$$

$$(3\text{-}2)$$

The first three independent variables quantify aspects of industry factor intensity. The scientists and engineers fraction is introduced to represent the relative importance of the product life cycle across industries. All variable definitions and sources are shown in Appendix Table A-1. The independent variables are briefly discussed below.

In measuring factor intensity both direct and total factor requirements, the latter computed with the aid of input-output tables, have been used by other investigators. The direct requirements approach is the logically correct approach if there is free and frictionless trade in material inputs. The total requirements approach is logically correct if there is no trade in material inputs. Neither of these strong positions is likely true as there is trade in intermediate inputs, but it is not frictionless because of transport costs, tariffs, and other barriers to trade. The direct requirements approach is chosen here because trade in intermediate inputs, though not frictionless, reduces any intermediate good disadvantages.

The capital-labor ratio is stressed in the current textbook treatment of the Heckscher-Ohlin theory because capital and labor are considered the two major factors of production. The ratio is defined as total assets net of depreciation divided by total employment, each averaged over the four years 1967 to 1970. Since the United States is considered capital abundant, its sign might be expected to be positive, but capital mobility internationally would lead one to expect its coefficient to be insignificant, while the Leontief results suggest a negative result is possible.

Labor skill is expected to be positively related to net trade position as the United States is relatively skilled labor abundant. Two variables represent variation in labor skill across industries. Work force median years of education is one measure, although it does not measure any human capital developed in nonschool settings such as on-the-job training. Actual average earnings might better measure labor skill as differences in earnings should reflect differences in human capital.[20] However, this variable may also measure other influences on wage determination, such as unionization or racial composition of the work force.

To meet the latter objection, a skill index is computed.[21] The proportions of industry employment accounted for by each of seven skill classes, ranging from professional and technical workers to laborers, are used as weights applied to economywide median annual earnings for each skill class to arrive at an "expected" annual earnings estimate for each industry, which is used here as a skill index. The use of economywide earnings figures should diminish the importance of market imperfection influences on the measurement of skill. Many of these influences are relatively industry-specific.

A natural resource dummy is included to capture any effect of the U.S. relative resource disadvantage on the pattern of U.S. trade in manufactures. Because sugar and petroleum have been omitted from our sample (see Chapter 1), the dummy takes a value of one only for the two basic metal industries, steel and nonferrous.[22] The United States is not likely to have a disadvantage vis-a-vis the rest of the world in the availability of nonmetallic minerals or agricultural raw materials.[23]

Scientists and engineers as a fraction of total employment are used to represent the research and development intensity of an industry. To the extent that R & D is devoted to developing new products, this variable should capture the relative importance of the product life cycle theory to the industry. R & D devoted to process improvement is also likely to give the United States a temporary comparative advantage based on superior technology. The scientists and engineers fraction is therefore expected to be positively related to net trade position.

By linearizing Equation 3-2, a functional form for estimation is obtained. Results of this estimation over the sample of seventy-one industries are presented in Table 3-1. Equations 1 through 3 have net trade position deflated by total trade as the dependent variable. Equations 4 through 6 have net trade position deflated by available supply as the dependent variable. The results differ between these sets of equations in the statistical importance attached to the specifically product life cycle variable relative to the general factor intensity variables.

Of the factor-intensity variables, the labor skill variables are positively related and highly significant. The natural resource dummy has the expected negative sign and is marginally significant in the trade-deflated net trade equations. The capital-labor ratio is insignificant.

The scientists and engineers fraction coefficient has the expected sign. The coefficient is marginally significant in the trade-deflated net trade equations if the factor-intensity variables are included. It is highly significant otherwise. Apparently the product life cycle theory, with its stress on research and development, does add to the explanatory power of the general factor-intensity variables, which represent the Heckscher-Ohlin bases of comparative advantage.

Tests of the joint significance of the three factor-intensity variables are presented in Table 3-2. The null hypothesis that these variables jointly add no significant explanatory power to the net trade equations is rejected at the 0.01 level for the trade-deflated net trade equations and at the 0.05 or 0.10 level, depending on the labor skill variable, for the supply-deflated net trade equations.

These results indicate that the Heckscher-Ohlin theory and the product life cycle theory should be considered complementary. Both theories are based in part on the relative abundance of skilled labor in the United States. Note also that the statistical results are somewhat sensitive to the specification of the model and to the measurement of labor skill.[24]

INTRAINDUSTRY TRADE: SPECIFICATIONS AND RESULTS

Intraindustry trade is the part of industry total trade that is not net trade. It may be measured as twice the lesser of exports or imports. Total trade and available supply each scale this variable for statistical analysis.[25]

Variables that affect the total volume of international trade tend also to affect the volume of intraindustry trade if these influences do not dictate a clear comparative advantage. From previous discussion,

$$\text{Intraindustry Trade} = f_2 \ (\text{Transportability, Advertising}$$
$$\text{Intensity, Scientists \& Engineers Fraction, FDI Intensity})$$

(3-3)

Results of estimation of a linearized version of this equation are presented in Table 3-3.[26] The explanatory power of both equations is poor.

The effect of transportability, measured by the 80 percent shipping radius, depends upon the choice of dependent variable. In relation to total trade, intraindustry trade is larger for less easily transported goods. The importance of border trade in these goods receives support. In relation to available supply, intraindustry trade is larger for more easily transported goods. This latter result probably is due to the larger total volume of trade in more easily transported goods.

Aspects of product differentiation are represented by advertising intensity and the scientists and engineers fraction. Apparently advertising, rather than representing product differentiation, acts predominantly as a barrier reducing both total and intraindustry trade. The effect of differentiability in increasing intraindustry trade may be evident in the positive relationship between the scientists and engineers fraction and supply-deflated intraindustry trade. The life cycles of various products of the high-technology industries may have progressed by the late 1960s to two-way trade. The United States presumably exports recently developed products and imports older, more standardized products.

FDI intensity is positively related to intraindustry trade. This result may reflect the role of FDI in the product life cycle or the use of offshore assembly plants by some industries. However, in a recent empirical examination of U.S. intraindustry trade, Pagoulatos and Sorensen hypothesize and find that FDI reduces intraindustry trade by reducing trade generally.[27] The results presented here question the robustness of their result.

The effects of transportability and of aspects of product differentiation on the extent of intraindustry trade have been explored and demonstrated empirically. However, the results are not satisfying. Many of the variables are only marginally significant. The total explanatory power of the equations is low. Using a more extensive data base, Pagoulatos and Sorensen obtained generally superior statistical results.[28]

Table 3-1. Net Trade Position Ordinary Least-Squares Regressions

Equation	1	2	3	4	5	6
Capital-Labor Ratio	0.310E-2 (0.79)	-0.180E-3 (0.05)	—	-0.395E-3 (0.85)	-0.605E-3 (1.24)	—
Skill Index	0.870E-3 (3.74)	—	—	0.789E-4 (2.90)	—	—
Median Years of Schooling	—	0.370 (3.91)	—	—	0.025 (2.19)	—
Natural Resource Dummy	-0.552 (1.68)	-0.470 (1.42)	—	-0.046 (1.18)	-0.040 (0.99)	—
Scientists & Engineers Fraction	2.978 (1.26)	3.116 (1.36)	8.852 (4.51)	0.705 (2.56)	0.837 (3.03)	1.146 (5.17)
Constant	-5.837 (3.93)	-4.407 (4.17)	-0.232 (2.81)	-0.523 (3.01)	-0.299 (2.34)	-0.030 (3.20)
$\bar{R}^2$	0.346	0.356	0.216	0.344	0.311	0.269

Dependent variable: Net Trade Position (Trade Deflated), equations 1, 2, 3.
Net Trade Position (Supply Deflated), equations 4, 5, 6.

Number of observations: 71.

t-statistics shown in parentheses. Significance levels for one-tailed $t(60)$ are:

0.10 : 1.30
0.05 : 1.67
0.01 : 2.39

Table 3-2.   Hypothesis Testing

This table presents results of tests of the joint influence of variables representing the Heckscher-Ohlin theory of comparative advantage. The null hypothesis is that three variables, the Capital-Labor Ratio, the Natural Resource Dummy, and either the Skill Index or Median Years of Schooling, jointly add no significant explanatory power to the equations of Table 3-1.

Human Capital Variable	Net Trade Position (Trade Deflated)	Net Trade Position (Supply Deflated)
Skill Index	5.55	3.58
Median Years of Schooling	6.00	2.35

These F-tests are based on equations 1, 2, 4, and 5 of Table 3-1. Degrees of freedom for each test are (3, 66).

Significance levels for $F(3, 60)$ are:

0.10 : 2.18
0.05 : 2.76
0.01 : 4.13

Table 3-3.   Intraindustry Trade Ordinary Least-Squares Regressions

Equation	1	2
Scientists & Engineers Fraction	−0.397 (0.31)	0.283 (1.53)
80% Shipping Radius	−0.115E-3 (1.31)	0.187E-4 (1.45)
Advertising Intensity	−3.604 (2.06)	−0.527 (2.05)
FDI Intensity	0.483 (1.63)	0.066 (1.51)
Constant	0.619 (7.58)	0.024 (2.04)
$\bar{R}^2$	0.045	0.141

Dependent variable: Intraindustry Trade (Trade Deflated), equation 1.
Intraindustry Trade (Supply Deflated), equation 2.

Number of observations: 71.

t-statistics shown in parentheses. Significance levels for one-tailed $t(60)$ are:

0.10 : 1.30
0.05 : 1.67
0.01 : 2.39

EXPORT AND IMPORT SHARES: SPECIFICATIONS AND RESULTS

This section explores the determinants of export share and import share separately, both to extend the analysis of comparative advantage and to test other hypotheses developed earlier in this chapter. Export share is defined as exports divided by shipments, that is, the fraction of U.S. production that is exported. Import share is defined as imports divided by shipments minus exports plus imports, that is, the fraction of apparent domestic consumption that is imported.

In addition to comparative advantage, the influences of ease of transportation and of advertising on both export and import shares are analyzed. The effects of domestic pricing and of government trade policy on import shares are also analyzed, although data limitations preclude analysis of these effects on export shares. Therefore,

Export Share = f_3 (Capital-Labor Ratio, Labor Skill,

Natural Resource Dummy, Scientists & Engineers

Fraction, 80% Shipping Radius, Advertising Intensity)　　(3-4)

and

Import Share = f_4 (Capital-Labor Ratio, Labor Skill,

Natural Resource Dummy, Scientists & Engineers

Fraction, 80% Shipping Radius, Advertising Intensity,

Before-Tax Profit/Sales, Tariff Rate, NTB, Quota)　　(3-5)

Each equation is linearized for estimation. Results of estimation of the export share are shown in Table 3-4. Results of estimation of the import share equation are shown in Table 3-5. Variable definitions and sources are given in Appendix Table A-1. The explanatory power of the export share equations is very good, but the explanatory power of the import share equations, especially on an adjusted basis, is rather poor.[29]

The comparative adantage variables were discussed in the section on net trade, pages 46 to 49. Analysis of their effects on export and import patterns separately are intriguing. The capital-labor ratio is insignificantly related to export share. It is significantly and positively related to import share, although its significance in the import share equation is often marginal. Capital-intensity apparently has an important influence only on the determination of the U.S. import pattern.

The labor skill variables generally have the expected coefficient signs, positive in the export share equations and negative in the import share equations. Both the skill index and median schooling are significant in the export share equations. Labor skill variables in the import share equations are beset by multicollinearity with the tariff

Table 3-4. Export Share Ordinary Least-Squares Regressions

Equation	1	2
Capital-Labor Ratio	0.211E-3 (0.62)	0.101E-3 (0.30)
Skill Index	0.381E-4 (1.91)	–
Median Years of Schooling	–	0.023 (2.68)
Natural Resource Dummy	−0.020 (0.73)	−0.020 (0.74)
Scientists & Engineers Fraction	0.706 (3.36)	0.588 (2.79)
80% Shipping Radius	0.344E-4 (2.72)	0.417E-4 (3.22)
Advertising Intensity	−0.391 (1.59)	−0.567 (2.32)
Constant	−0.246 (1.89)	−0.262 (2.64)
$\bar{R}^2$	0.460	0.487

Dependent variable: Export Share.

Number of observations: 71.

t-statistics are shown in parentheses. Significance levels for one-tailed $t(60)$ are:

$$0.10 : 1.30$$
$$0.05 : 1.67$$
$$0.01 : 2.39$$

rate variables.[30] The skill index is significant in equation 1 and 3, but insignificant in equation 2, which includes the nominal tariff rate. The education variable is never significant. Labor skill is a significant determinant of both export and import patterns, although this result is not robust in import share equations for measurement of labor skill.

The coefficient of the natural resource dummy is insignificant in all equations, although its sign is consistent with a resource-based disadvantage in the basic metals industries.

The scientists and engineers fraction, included to represent product life cycle influences, is positively related and highly significant in the export share equations, but insignificant in the import share equations. Research and development activity is important in explaining the U.S. export pattern, but not the import pattern.

Transportability, as measured by the 80 percent shipping radius, is a significant determinant of both export share and import share. Relative to industry size, more easily transported goods tend to be traded more.

Advertising intensity is posited to represent two influences. It may represent the relative importance of product differentiation across industries. Both exports and imports could be larger due to product differentiation because foreign firms can secure market niches supplied by their own peculiar products. But relatively high advertising intensity may require foreign producers to promote their own brand in order to secure sales. Advertising may act as a barrier to trade if foreign producers forgo risky marketing investments. The coefficient on advertising is negative and significant in the export share equations and negative but usually insignificant in the import share equations. Advertising acts predominanly as a barrier to trade in the same way that it acts as a domestic entry barrier.

The effect of profitability on the incentive to import could not be shown. Its coefficient is always insignificant in Table 3-5. Because import competition was hypothesized as a determiant of profitability in Chapter 2, the results reported here may suffer from simultaneous equations bias. A discussion of this issue and additional results will be presented in the next chapter. In two-stage least-squares estimation presented there, increased profitability does tend to increase import share, other things being equal.

The effect of the nominal tariff rate on the import share cannot be isolated due to collinearity with the labor skill variables. The political process in the United States grants relatively greater tariff protection to industries intensive in unskilled labor.[31] The collinearity overpowers the expected import-reducing effect of the nominal tariff rate.[32]

Nontariff barriers (NTBs) are measured as the percentage of imports affected by nontariff barriers, drawing upon estimates developed by Walter.[33] Unfortunately, the concordance between his industries and the IRS industries used in this study is poor. Nontariff barriers impede imports, but this result is not significant across industries. Perhaps the only way to effectively study NTBs is industry by industry as their incidence is very difficult to quantify and summarize across industries.

A dummy is used to indicate those industries whose imports were affected by quotas, whether imposed by the United States or "voluntarily" by foreign governments, during this period. The two most affected industries, sugar (IRS 2060) and petroleum (IRS 2910), are dropped entirely from the sample. Industries receiving a quota dummy value of one are all textile and apparel industries (IRS 2228, 2250, 2298, 2310, 2330, 2380, and 2398) and dairy products (IRS 2020).[34] Steel (IRS 3310) is not included in the quota industries although the United States did negotiate a global steel exporting agreement, which took effect in 1969. Mintz concluded that many countries did not fill

Table 3-5. Import Share Ordinary Least-Squares Regressions

Equation	1	2	3	4	5	6
Capital-Labor Ratio	0.529E-3 (1.35)	0.875E-3 (2.09)	0.462E-3 (1.17)	0.560E-3 (1.39)	0.964E-3 (2.34)	0.530E-3 (1.30)
Skill Index	-0.409E-4 (1.74)	-0.228E-4 (0.86)	-0.501E-4 (2.00)	—	—	—
Median Years of Schooling	—	—	—	-0.531E-2 (0.50)	0.480E-2 (0.42)	-0.829E-2 (0.71)
Natural Resource Dummy	0.029 (0.92)	0.025 (0.82)	0.027 (0.85)	0.028 (0.86)	0.023 (0.76)	0.026 (0.81)
Scientists & Engineers Fraction	0.022 (0.09)	-0.104 (0.42)	0.069 (0.28)	-0.156 (0.62)	-0.295 (1.21)	-0.117 (0.45)
80% Shipping Radius	0.315E-4 (2.14)	0.342E-4 (2.38)	0.316E-4 (2.15)	0.366E-4 (2.29)	0.406E-4 (2.65)	0.359E-4 (2.22)
Advertising Intensity	-0.239 (0.78)	-0.490 (1.57)	-0.216 (0.71)	-0.130 (0.42)	-0.498 (1.56)	-0.094 (0.30)
Before-Tax Profit Sales	-0.734E-2 (0.04)	-0.112 (0.61)	-0.015 (0.09)	-0.066 (0.36)	-0.184 (0.95)	-0.068 (0.37)
Nominal Tariff	—	0.252 (2.59)	—	—	0.296 (3.05)	—
NTB	—	-0.132E-2 (0.08)	—	—	-0.212E-2 (0.13)	—

	(1)	(2)	(3)	(4)	(5)	(6)
Quota	—	-0.037 (1.74)	—	—	-0.033 (1.55)	—
Effective Tariff	—	—	-0.032 (1.07)	—	—	-0.021 (0.65)
Constant	0.280 (1.84)	0.145 (0.82)	0.346 (2.11)	0.077 (0.63)	-0.062 (0.46)	0.116 (0.85)
$\bar{R}^2$	0.102	0.160	0.104	0.063	0.152	0.054

Dependent variable: Import Share.

Number of observations: 71.

t-statistics are shown in parentheses. Significance levels for one-tailed $t(60)$ are:

0.10 : 1.30
0.05 : 1.67
0.01 : 2.39

their quota in either 1969 or 1970 due to strong demand outside of the United States.[35] Therefore the steel quota is treated as nonbinding during these years. The coefficient on this quota dummy is negative and significant.

The joint significance of the three governmental policy variables in equations 2 and 5 of Table 3-5 may be tested. *F*-statistics with 3 and 60 degrees of freedom for the null hypothesis that these three variables add no significant explanatory power to each of the equations are 2.43 and 3.21, respectively. The null hypothesis is rejected at the 0.10 and 0.05 level, respectively. These results indicate that the governmental policy variables are not significant merely because of collinearity with the skill variables, but add significant information to the estimation.

Effective tariff rates were calculated by Baldwin for 1964 and 1972.[36] These rates include some nontariff barriers. A simple average of the two rates yields a measure applicable to the years of our study. Unfortunately a serious concordance problem is also encountered in moving from Baldwin's industries to the IRS industries. Although the effective tariff rate is negatively related to import share, as expected, its coefficient is insignificant.

The results of analyzing export and import share separately are informative although the performance of the import share regressions is somewhat disappointing. Implications for theories of comparative advantage are developed in the next section. Other influences have been explored. The importance of transportability to international trade flows has been demonstrated. The importance of barriers to import through advertising and governmental fiat has been indicated.[37]

COMPARATIVE ADVANTAGE: CONCLUSIONS

In the section on net trade, pages 46 to 49, tests of significance of factor-intensity and product life cycle variables indicated that both sets of influences are important in explaining the U.S. net trade pattern. The complementarity of Heckscher-Ohlin and product life cycle theories of comparative advantage was further demonstrated in the analysis of export and import patterns in the previous section.

Labor skill is an important determinant of both patterns as the Heckscher-Ohlin theory predicts. The variable representing research and development intensity was significant only in explaining export patterns. This result is consistent with the product life cycle theory. The United States is a leader in developing new products and technologies. Owing to a monopoly of knowledge, the United States exports these products. The research and development aspects of the product life cycle theory are not predicted to influence the U.S. import pattern.

The capital-labor ratio was significant only in the determination of the import pattern. Since it is positively related to import share, the result is not consistent with Heckscher-Ohlin theory. The product life cycle theory, however, states that production in the mature phase of the cycle is relatively capital-intensive. The theory is consistent with the capital-labor result because the United States generally has a comparative disadvantage during the mature phase.

Another set of influences may be partially responsible for this result. Taxation of export profits varies widely across countries. The United States in the late 1960s taxed export profits at nearly the same rate as profit on domestic sales.[38] This period was pre-DISC (Domestic International Sales Corporations). The United States enforces strict transfer pricing rules between domestic parents and foreign subsidiaries, thus lessening the advantages of tax haven subsidiaries. Export profits in most other countries (Canada and West Germany are possible exceptions) are taxed at substantially lower rates than domestic profits.[39] These lower taxes are achieved by liberal transfer pricing rules allowing profits to be shown in tax haven conduit subsidiaries, whose profits are then lightly taxed by the parent country government as well. Foreign tax policies usually encourage exporting, and the incentive is a positive function of the industry capital-intensity (through its relation to the profit per unit of sales). The foreign tax structures therefore tend to distort the import pattern of the United States. Any foreign governmental influence on capital rationing or implicit subsidization favoring capital-intensive export industries reinforces this distortion.

Taken as a whole, the results of the separate export and import share analysis lend support to both the product life cycle and Heckscher-Ohlin relative labor-skill theories of trade. Indeed it seems best to accept the complementarity of the two theories as explanations of the pattern of U.S. trade. The product life cycle theory adds important dynamic elements to the more static Heckscher-Ohlin considerations.[40] The results of this chapter also indicate the importance of frictional factors in affecting the pattern of trade.

NOTES

1. R.M. Stern, "Testing Trade Theories," in Peter B. Kenen, ed., *International Trade and Finance: Frontiers For Research*, 1975.

2. J.F. Morrall III, *Human Capital, Technology, and the Role of the United States in International Trade*, 1972.

3. E. Heckscher, "The Effect of Foreign Trade on the Distribution of Income," *Economisk Tidskrift*, 1919, and Bertil Ohlin, *Interregional and International Trade*, 1933.

4. W.W. Leontief, "Domestic Production and Foreign Trade: The American Capital Position Re-examined," *Economia Internazionale*, February 1954.

5. D.B. Keesing, "Labor Skills and International Trade: Evaluating Many Trade Flows with a Single Measuring Device," *Review of Economics and Statistics*, August 1965.

6. S. Naya, "Natural Resources, Factor Mix, and Factor Reversal in International Trade," *American Economic Review*, May 1967.

7. *International Economic Report of the President*, 1975, pp. 22-29.

8. M.J. Peck, *Competition in the Aluminum Industry, 1945-1958*, 1961, ch. 2.

9. R. Vernon, "International Investment and International Trade in the Product Cycle," *Quarterly Journal of Economics*, May 1966; W. Gruber, D. Mehta, and R. Vernon, "The R & D Factor in International Trade and International Investment of United States Industries," *Journal of Political Economy*, February 1967; and L.T. Wells, Jr., "Test of a Product Cycle Model of International Trade: U.S. Exports of Consumer Durables," *Quarterly Journal of Economics*, February 1969.

10. W.P. Travis, "Production, Trade, and Protection When There Are Many Commodities and Two Factors," *American Economic Review*, March 1972.

11. Data limitations preclude analysis of the effects of foreign tariffs on U.S. exports.

12. I. Mintz, *U.S. Import Quotas: Costs and Consequences*, 1973.

13. R.E. Baldwin, *Nontariff Distortions of International Trade*, 1970.

14. H.G. Grubel and P.J. Lloyd, *Intra-industry Trade*, 1975.

15. A. Auquier has pointed out that EEC exporting activities tend to be dominated by the larger EEC firms.

16. E. Pagoulatos and R. Sorensen, "Domestic Market Structure and International Trade: An Empirical Analysis," *Quarterly Review of Economics and Business*, Spring 1976, fail to make this distinction.

17. W.H. Branson and H.B. Junz, "Trends in U.S. Trade and Comparative Advantage," *Brookings Papers on Economic Activity*, no. 2, 1971, did not scale the net trade dependent variable. W.H. Branson, "U.S. Comparative Advantage: Some Further Results," *Brookings Papers on Economic Activity*, no. 3, 1971, presents similar empirical work using net trade deflated by total trade as the dependent variable. Scaling improved the results.

18. Each of these variables has a potential range of -1.0 to 1.0. If scaling were done by domestic shipments or apparent domestic consumption, the potential ranges would have been $-\infty$ to 1.0 or -1.0 to ∞, respectively. Scaling by available supply was chosen to avoid these asymmetrical potential ranges.

19. Because the variable may be either negative or positive, there is no simple statistical method to control for ease of transportation.

20. G.S. Becker, *Human Capital*, second edition, 1975, ch. II.

21. Based on the method developed by A.W. Throop, "The Union-Nonunion Wage Differential and Cost-Push Inflation," *American Economic Review*, March 1968.

22. Branson and Junz found that results in a similar analysis did not change when the basic metals sectors were eliminated. Here the dummy should pick up any differences in levels caused by the natural resource disadvantage.

23. H. Baumann, "Structural Characteristics of Canada's Pattern of Trade," *Canadian Journal of Economics*, August 1976, found that Canadian comparative advantage vis-a-vis the United States was based on general raw material availability. Relative to the rest of the world rather than just Canada, however, the United States is not likely to have a general natural resource availability disadvantage.

24. T.C. Lowinger, "The Technology Factor and the Export Performance of U.S. Manufacturing Industries," *Economic Inquiry*, June 1975, concluded that the product life cycle theory was superior to the skilled labor advantage hypothesis of Heckscher-Ohlin theory. However, his measure of labor intensity was total wages and salaries divided by value added. This variable fails to distinguish between simple labor intensity and skilled labor intensity. It is not surprising that the explanatory power of the Heckscher-Ohlin theory is not robust to poor variable definition.

25. The range of each of these variables is 0.0 to 1.0. H.G. Grubel, "Intra-Industry Specialization and the Pattern of Trade," *Canadian Journal of Economics and Political Science*, August 1967, deflated by total trade.

26. Attempts to determine the influence of economies of scale produced insignificant results. Economies of scale were represented by minimum efficient scale of plant relative to the market and the cost-disadvantage ratio of small-scale production.

27. E. Pagoulatos and R. Sorensen, "Two-Way International Trade: An Econometric Analysis," *Weltwirtschaftliches Archiv*, 1975.

28. Pagoulatos and Sorensen, "Two-Way International Trade: An Econometric Analysis."

29. In a similar empirical analysis H. Baumann explained very little of the cross-industry variation in the Canadian export pattern to the United States (R^2 reported as 0.206 or less).

30. Between the skill index and the nominal tariff, $r = 0.479$. Between the schooling variable and the nominal tariff, $r = 0.393$. The correlations with the effective tariff rate are slightly lower.

31. This result was noted by J.H. Cheh, "A Note on Tariffs, Non-Tariff Barriers, and Labor Protection in United States Manufacturing Industries," *Journal of Political Economy*, April 1976; and David Stafford Ball, "United States Effective Tariffs and Labor's Share," *Journal of Political Economy*, April 1967.

32. A further attempt to isolate the impact of the tariff rate uses a split variable, Nominal Tariff Low, which has a value equal to the Nominal Tariff if it is less than or equal to 0.10 and zero otherwise, and Nominal Tariff High, which has a value equal to the Nominal Tariff if it is greater than 0.10 and zero otherwise. Equations 2 and 5 of Table 3-5 are reestimated. The coefficients on Nominal Tariff Low are −0.074 and −0.040, respectively, but each coefficient is less than half its standard error. The coefficients on Nominal Tariff High are 0.219 and 0.257, respectively. Each is significant. The coefficients and t-statistics of the skill variables are little affected.

33. I. Walter, "Non-Tariff Protection Among Industrial Countries: Some Preliminary Evidence," *Economia Internazionale*, May 1972.

34. Mintz.

35. Mintz, pp. 79-83.

36. Baldwin.

37. Attempts to measure the influence of economies of scale using various minimum efficient scale of plant variables produced no significant results. Past results for the influence of economies of scale on the U.S. net trade position are mixed. Branson and Junz and Branson obtained insignificant results. L. Weiser and K. Jay, "Determinants of the Commodity Structure of U.S. Trade: Comment," *American Economic Review*, June 1972, obtained significant results.

38. Western Hemisphere Trading Corporations could, however, be used to lower taxation of profits on goods exported by U.S. firms to Western Hemisphere countries during this period.

39. Gary C. Hufbauer, "The Taxation of Export Profits," *National Tax Journal*, March 1975; and Thomas Horst, *Income Taxation and Competitiveness in the United States, West Germany, France, The United Kingdom, and Japan*, 1977.

40. J.F. Morrall III, *Human Capital, Technology, and the Role of the United States in International Trade*, 1972, agrees with this conclusion based on his 2-digit cross-sectional analysis. However, by examining various data on wage variation across countries, he notes that while the United States is quantity-abundant in skilled labor, it appears to be price-abundant in unskilled labor. He then concludes that any Heckscher-Ohlin explanation of the U.S. trade pattern cannot be correct and accepts the product life cycle as the only major theory capable of explaining the trade pattern. However, his conclusion seems too strong, for in a hybrid theory incorporating both Heckscher-Ohlin and product life cycle components, differing technologies and dynamic considerations would indicate that one cannot expect static Heckscher-Ohlin price abundance to hold at any given point in time.

❋   *Chapter 4*

A Structural Model of
Industrial Product Markets

The preceding chapters considered the determinants of U.S. manufacturing industries' pricing and profits and of the U.S. commodity pattern of trade in manufactures. The importance of international trade influences on domestic pricing and profitability and the effects of certain aspects of market structure and market conduct on the pattern of trade were demonstrated using ordinary least-squares (OLS) estimation. However, problems of simultaneity are evident in these relationships. OLS is not an unbiased estimation method. To overcome the problems of simultaneity, this chapter develops a structural model of manufactured good product markets in long-run equilibrium. This model is estimated using an unbiased technique, two-stage least squares (TSLS).

Three equations of the system already were discussed, the profitability, export share, and import share equations. Three more equations are developed. Discussion of the market structure and market conduct determinants of the pattern of the U.S. outward foreign direct investment (FDI) broadens and concludes the analysis of the interrelationships among market structure, market conduct, international trade, and international investment. The determinants of advertising intensity and concentration are developed to complete the model of manufactured good product markets. Alternative specifications of this model are then discussed and estimated.

Two methodological conclusions are reached on the basis of estimation of the individual equations as a system. Only a few of the OLS coefficients are seriously biased. The inefficiency of TSLS relative to OLS is slight for carefully specified structural models.

FOREIGN DIRECT INVESTMENT

Chapter 3 analyzed the pattern of international trade across manufacturing industries. This section analyzes the relative importance of foreign direct investment across these industries and discusses the relations between trade and foreign direct investment.

Foreign direct investment (FDI) is defined as a capital movement from a home country to a host country that creates a substantial, usually controlling, equity interest in a host country corporate entity. For our purposes capital movements to establish an unincorporated branch of a home country corporate parent are also considered foreign direct investment. These unincorporated branches are relatively unimportant to manufacturing foreign direct investment.[1]

This section analyzes foreign direct investment of the United States as the home country. Data on FDI into the United States is less readily available in a form consistent with the method of analysis used here.[2]

A number of welfare issues arise in relation to FDI. For the United States, most concern has been with the aggregate effects of outward FDI on employment, labor earnings growth, and gross national product growth. Recently, Bergsten, Horst, and Moran hypothesized a feedback impact of outward FDI on competition and allocative efficiency in U.S. product markets.[3] A better understanding of these issues may result from an analysis of the determinants of FDI.

The original theories of foreign direct investment developed as an outgrowth of international portfolio capital theory. Countries with relatively abundant capital and relatively low interest rates tend to export capital to high interest rate countries, assuming that international trade in commodities does not equalize factor returns. Foreign direct investment is merely one channel through which this international redistribution of capital occurs. This theory might be sufficient if FDI were relatively unimportant, but the importance of and rapid growth of foreign direct investment in this century leaves the theory inadequate. If interest rate differentials are the only important factor, establishment of control over production activities abroad is unnecessary. Control indeed reduces returns if the foreign owner is at a disadvantage because of lack of knowledge of local customs, laws, and business practices. Stephen Hymer offered an alternative theory based on market structure and conduct.[4] Richard Caves, among others, has extended and refined the theory.[5]

Foreign direct investment is usually industry-specific. Horizontal FDI, in which the subsidiary produces the same products as the parent, and vertical FDI, in which the subsidiary provides raw material inputs to the parent, processes components for the parent, or establishes sales and service organizations for the parent's products, predominate the total of foreign direct investment. Conglomerate FDI, in which the subsidiary produces products substantially different from any produced by the parent, is relatively unimportant though increasing.[6] Therefore, aspects of the markets within which the parent or the subsidiary operate are important in analyzing the pattern of foreign direct investment.

Parent firms considering a horizontal foreign direct investment are likely at a disadvantage relative to local producers. The parent firm lacks knowledge of local laws, customs, market channels, favored promotional strategies, and other types of information generally taken for granted or obtained by local firms at low cost, but costly for the parent firm to obtain. The parent firm may also face actual or potential host government discrimination. The parent firm must possess other assets that allow it to overcome these disadvantages if foreign direct investment is to be successful. Furthermore, these assets must be available to the parent firm for use in the host country at sufficiently low cost to make the operation profitable.

Use of intangible assets offers the parent firm a means to overcome local disadvantages. Knowledge of successful product promotion techniques or registered brand names are assets that can be used in foreign markets without diminishing their value or productivity in the home market. Exclusive product or process knowledge based on the research and development (R & D) activity of the parent firm can also be exploited in foreign markets. The need to adapt products and promotional techniques to local demand characteristics may require that local production and marketing facilities be established to fully exploit these assets.

Other intangible assets available for use in FDI activity are organizational skills. These skills result in a higher productivity of management personnel. U.S. firms may have an advantage over foreign rivals in their use of management abilities.[7] A U.S. firm may establish a foreign subsidiary to exploit simultaneously its advantage in organization and local advantages in other aspects of production as the cost of unskilled or semiskilled labor. Expatriate management personnel are used at first, but often foreign managers are trained to replace them. The advantage of the U.S. firm is based on its skill in organizing and motivating its management.

A third kind of asset potentially available to the firm is its ability to raise capital and undertake risk. The capital barrier is especially important in projects of relatively large size. A firm with an entrenched home market position and sufficient size to absorb the risk is at an advantage over host country firms as a potential entrant into markets characterized by high-entry barriers (barriers discussed in Chapter 2).

Knickerbocker has suggested that oligopolistic interdependence among home country firms may induce all to move quickly into a market when any one does. Imitative behavior occurs to maintain foreign market position or to preclude any one firm from gaining a competitive advantage not obvious prior to initial entry.[8]

The discussion suggests that horizontal FDI is likely to be relatively more important in industries characterized by relatively high product differentiation, relatively high research and development intensity, relatively intensive use of management skills, relatively high capital requirements for minimum efficient scale production, and relatively high home market producer concentration. Some of these influences indicate assets available to the investor for exploitation in the host country markets. Others indicate either the ability to undertake FDI or home market forces acting upon the decision to undertake FDI.

One important form of vertical foreign direct investment is backward to secure sources of supply of raw materials.[9] Besides reducing uncertainty as to supply,[10] the investment often raises an absolute cost barrier to the entry of new firms in the home country market.[11] This type of FDI is likely prevalent in natural resource-based industries in which the sources of supply of the resource are either very limited or of widely ranging quality.

A firm possessing assets that yield a return in a foreign market may exploit those assets by exporting, foreign direct investment production, or licensing. The difficulty of negotiating an agreeable price given the uncertainty of the asset's return or the fear of developing a potentially strong rival usually makes licensing relatively unattractive for all but small firms who lack the necessary capital and the ability to undertake the risk inherent in the establishment of a foreign subsidiary. If licensing is precluded, the firm faces a choice between exporting and FDI production. Some vertical FDI forward into sales and service facilitates exporting. This sales subsidiary may also act as a stepping-stone to full local production facilities as it is used to gather local information and develop a local market for the firm's products.

The firm's decision between exporting and FDI production is based on considerations discussed in the preceding chapter. Comparative advantage, as reflected in both relative production costs and relative material input costs, transport costs, and tariffs influence the relative profitability of the two means of supplying foreign markets. The need to adapt the product to the local market may be important.

Economies of scale in production also influence the choice. In the absence of significant frictions acting on exports, production characterized by scale economies is concentrated in a few locations, although perhaps it is located on a historical development basis rather than efficiently located according to comparative advantage. But the erection of tariff barriers to trade allow and perhaps force local, small-scale, relatively inefficient production behind these walls to safeguard the parent firm's market position.[12]

This discussion suggests that exporting and FDI may be either complementary (through sales subsidiaries) or competing. An attempt to isolate these relationships was successful in considering United States-Canada decisions, where tariffs and relative market sizes (a proxy for scale economy effects) were shown to influence the interindustry variation in export to export plus subsidiary sales ratios, but less successful in analyzing United States-United Kingdom and United States-EEC exporting and FDI behavior.[13] Efforts to isolate the overall relation between U.S. exports and U.S. outward FDI were unsuccessful, owing to collinearity between the determinants of the two and inadequate data to overcome this collinearity.[14]

Foreign direct investment may also influence U.S. imports. Subsidiaries set up abroad based on comparative advantage may be favored as exporters to the United States because of their access to parents' marketing facilities. In addition, component processing plants are established abroad to accept parts from the U.S. parent or other subsidiaries and to export semifinished or finished goods to the U.S. parent. The importance of these FDI-import relations has not been established empirically.

A model of the pattern of FDI across indusstries has been developed, suggesting that

FDI Intensity = f (Advertising Intensity, Scientists &

Engineers Fraction, Managers Fraction, Natural Resource

Dummy, Cost-adjusted Capital Requirements, C4)   (4-1)

This model is linearized for estimation as significant interactive effects are not evident.[15] The variables used in estimation are defined in Table A-1. The variable FDI intensity and problems inherent in its measurement are discussed in Appendix 4-1. OLS regression results are presented in Table 4-1.

Intangible assets are hypothesized to lend themselves especially well to exploitation through foreign direct investment. Assets associated with product differentiation are indicated by the advertising intensity of the industry. While advertising does not capture such aspects of product differentiation as the ability and willingness to customize or provide special services, it does capture two important aspects of product differentiation, product branding and mass

Table 4-1.   FDI Ordinary Least-Squares Regressions

Equation	1	2
Advertising Intensity	1.344	1.136
	(2.03)	(1.63)
Scientists & Engineers	1.433	1.402
Fraction	(3.39)	(3.01)
Managers Fraction	1.460	1.263
	(2.21)	(1.84)
Natural Resource Dummy	0.186	0.176
	(2.57)	(2.30)
C4 (3-digit)	0.220	–
	(2.90)	
C4 (4-digit)	–	0.182
		(1.98)
Cost-adjusted	−0.157E-4	0.310E-7
Capital Requirements	(0.79)	(0.00)
Constant	−0.078	−0.103
	(1.81)	(1.90)
$\bar{R}^2$	0.407	0.368

Dependent variable: FDI Intensity.

Number of observations: 71.

t-statistics shown in parentheses. Significance levels for a one-tailed $t(60)$ are:

$$0.10 : 1.30$$
$$0.05 : 1.67$$
$$0.01 : 2.39$$

marketing skills. This variable is positive and significant in both equations, replicating similar results obtained in studies by Caves[16] and Horst.[17]

A second major intangible asset is knowledge obtained through research and development. The research and development intensity of an industry is indicated by the fraction of scientists and engineers in total employment. This variable is positive and significant in both regressions, again replicating results of Caves[18] and Horst.[19]

A managerial advantage is hypothesized favoring U.S.-based firms over local firms. This advantage may be based on superior U.S. organizational skills. Caves attempted to test this by identifying variables that indicate the complexity of the management function within the industry.[20] His variables, percentage nonproduction workers in total employment and measures of earnings per employee, seem equally related to U.S. comparative advantage, however, and his results were insignificant. Here the fraction of managers in total employment is taken as a direct indicator of the importance of the management function across industries. It is positive and significant, indicating that the U.S. advantage in management and organizational skills is an important U.S. asset exploited through FDI.

Large firms in secure market positions are hypothesized to have access to capital at favorable rates, perhaps reflecting their risk-pooling abilities. Favorable access makes them favored entrants into markets requiring large absolute capital expenditures to construct a plant of minimum efficient scale. However, these same economies of scale compel firms to centralize production if possible. Economies of scale tend to slow the locational aspects of the product life cycle and favor exporting over FDI. Cost-adjusted capital requirements are negatively related, though not significant, in equation 1. Large minimum efficient scale weakly deters FDI. Perhaps the capital cost advantages are small.

Home market concentration may encourage FDI because of risk-pooling abilities, favored entrant status into similarly structured foreign markets, and oligopolistic reaction. It is positive and significant in all regressions.[21]

The positive and significant results obtained with the natural resource dummy support the contention that backward vertical integration, which acts as a domestic barrier to entry, is important in these resource-intensive industries. While Horst treats wood, paper, nonmetallic mineral products, and basic metals as natural resource industries,[22] the dummy used here refers only to basic metals (steel and nonferrous). U.S. comparative disadvantage in timber production is not apparent, although this factor may be relevant to U.S. FDI in Canada. Indeed, Horst found his variable significant in explaining U.S. FDI in Canada but not in the world as a whole. The nonmetallic mineral industries (glass, cement, concrete, gypsum, plaster, clay, and other nonmetallic mineral products, IRS 3210, 3240, 3270, and 3298) require raw materials more geographically widespread than the metals industries. Entry barriers into these industries are not so easily erected through control of raw material sources.

Finally, the attempt to isolate the impact of FDI on U.S. exports and imports is not successful.[23] Both variables are insignificant, and export share is positively related to FDI. These results are not reported. Data on intracorporation international goods transactions at a sufficiently disaggregated level would be useful in analyzing these relationships.

The results support many of the theories presented earlier. They substantiate the view that FDI activity should be considered industry-specific. In particular, the results uphold intangible asset theories based on product differentiation or research and development activity. Support is found for the theory that U.S. firms may be favored entrants into high-entry barrier foreign markets, as advertising intensity and market concentration tend to enhance FDI activity, although large minimum efficient scale of plant, the basis for other entry barriers, may deter FDI. Knickerbocker's theory of the importance of oligopolistic reaction in firms' FDI decisions receives indirect support through the positive relation between FDI and concentration.[24] The role of management efficiency or organizational skill advantages of U.S. firms is also demonstrated.

Foreign direct investment by U.S. firms and their ability to export are shown to rest on similar U.S. comparative advantage as posited by the product life cycle theory of trade and investment. Although the interrelations between trade and FDI are not fully demonstrated, Caves's proposition that FDI tends to go where trade cannot receives support in the findings. Advertising intensity, which was shown to be a barrier to trade in Chapter 3, is here shown to be a significant, positively related determinant of relative FDI activity across industries.[25]

ADVERTISING INTENSITY

Advertising intensity was tested as a determinant of pricing, trade patterns, and FDI. This section explores the determinants of advertising intensity, an important aspect of market conduct.

Advertising is primarily intended to communicate information, whether it be "hard" information, such as availability, price, or uses, or "soft" information, such as the images developed to accompany use of the product. Primary determinants of advertising intensity thus are the purchasers of the good, both in their demand for information and in their receptivity to information communicated in this format.

Most advertising is expected to be directed to household consumers. Household consumers make many decisions about goods purchases and likely possess little technical expertise in judging a wide range of these products. Producer purchases, except perhaps for purchases of some supplies, are usually relatively large, and buyers in these markets often acquire the technical expertise needed to judge the competing claims of rival products. Thus, advertising is likely more important in conveying information to household consumers, who may rely on advertising not because of the accuracy of the information conveyed but because of the relatively higher costs, whether money, time, or psychic costs, of alternative sources of information. Direct methods utilizing technically competent salespeople are likely more important in selling producer goods, both material inputs and capital goods. In addition, the relatively ill-defined nature of some household consumer wants to be satisfied by their product purchases makes specific information of less use.

However, not all products purchased by households are equally differentiable by manufacturer advertising. A distinction is often made between consumer durables and nondurables.[26] Durables are advertised less, perhaps because the infrequency of purchase and the inability to target consumers considering immediate purchase renders the cost effectiveness of advertising relatively lower. Porter has developed a separate though related distinction.[27] Goods are distinguished by the type of retail outlet through which they are sold. Convenience goods are sold through multiproduct stores such as grocery supermarkets or discount department stores. Nonconvenience goods are sold through smaller, usually single-product stores, such as audio equipment stores, automobile dealerships, or shoe stores. This categorization distinguishes the role of manufacturer advertising from retailer sales effort in establishing product differentiation and the appeal of different brands. Convenience good stores typically add little beyond the allocation of shelf space to the differentiation of brands of a particular product. Manufacturers through advertising must establish and promote their own brand. In the nonconvenience outlet the sales efforts of the outlet are more important to the final consumer decision. Typical manufacturers of nonconvenience goods are likely to split their promotion efforts between advertising directed toward the consumer and inducements offered to the retailer to improve retailer promotion of the manufacturers' brands.

The product and its potential purchasers are a primary determinant of advertising intensity. A number of other influences can be identified. The state of producer competition in a particular market may affect advertising intensity. If concentration is low and the product is essentially homogeneous, the rewards of advertising are difficult to appropriate by any one producer. As concentration rises, appropriability also becomes easier, and defensive advertising, which may be nearly self-canceling in its effects on consumer choice, may also become important. However, this defensive advertising need not be completely unproductive to the firms for it likely raises the barrier to entry of new firms. As concentration approaches very high levels, mutual interdependence may lead to effective tacit collusion to restrict advertising to jointly optimal levels. The advertising-concentration relation is hypothesized to be nonlinear. Advertising intensity at first increases with increasing producer concentration but then falls, other things being equal.[28]

The average age of the products in an industry and the frequency of new product or new brand introduction may influence the equilibrium level of advertising intensity.[29] Newer products are more advertised relative to their level of sales, both because the basic information of availability and potential uses must be conveyed and because a first purchase of the new product requires breaking the inertia of habit. The importance of new product development to an industry is represented by the research and development intensity of the industry. While R & D activity in an industry may be devoted to either process or product development, and only the latter should affect advertising, in consumer goods industries product development is predominant.

At least part of the advertising decision may be made in a residual manner after all other costs are covered in the plan for production and marketing.[30] Profitability may be a determinant of advertising. Firms earning large profits relative to their invested capital may decide that a part of these funds be used to expand advertising expenditure in an effort to solidify and perhaps even expand their market position.

A model of the equilibrium level of advertising intensity is developed that depends on the characteristics of the typical purchaser (e.g., household consumers), the product (e.g., consumer nonconvenience goods or new products), the sellers' market structure (concentration), and the availability of funds to engage in advertising. For empirical testing, we may formalize the model:

$$\text{Advertising Intensity} = f\,(\text{Consumer Demand, Nonconvenience Good Dummy, Scientists \& Engineers Fraction,}$$
$$C4, (C4)^2, \text{Excess Profit/Sales}) \qquad (4\text{-}2)$$

A durable consumer good dummy is sometimes used in place of the nonconvenience good dummy. The scientists and engineers fraction represents the R & D intensity of the industry. Excess profit is measured before taxes. Because advertising is immediately expensed in computing corporate income taxes, the government can be considered to pay for some fraction of an extra dollar of advertising. Firms thus may make the residual part of their advertising decision on the basis of before-tax profitability. All variable definitions and sources are given in Table A-1. Table A-2 presents lists of industries considered to market consumer nonconvenience goods or durable goods.

One specification for estimation is obtained by linearizing Equation 4-2. However, this linear specification may not correctly capture the influence of the independent variables on advertising intensity. The purchaser is the principal determinant of advertising intensity. All other influences act to modify this basic relationship. This proposition can be seen most easily in considering the influence of R & D intensity. R & D activity in producer goods industries is not expected to affect the equilibrium, very low level of advertising intensity. R & D in consumer goods industries is likely to affect advertising intensity levels across these industries through its relation to new product introduction.

These interactive effects are captured in the specification.[31]

Advertising Intensity = $a + b_1$ (CD · Nonconvenience

Good Dummy) + b_2 (CD · Scientists & Engineers

Fraction) + b_3 (CD · C4) + b_4 (CD · $(C4)^2$) + b_5

(CD · Excess Profit/Sales)   (4-3)

where CD is consumer demand. The interactive and noninteractive specifications are combined in

$$\text{Advertising Intensity} = a + \sum_i (a_i + b_i CD) X_i \qquad (4\text{-}4)$$

where the X_i are the five variables Nonconvenience Good Dummy through Excess Profit/Sales in Equation 4-2. Only results of tests of the joint significance of the a_i and b_i are reported here.

Results of estimation of the noninteractive specification are shown as equations 1 and 2 of Tables 4-2 and 4-3. Results of estimation of the interactive specification, Equation 4-3, are shown as equations 3 and 4 of these tables. The results generally support the hypotheses of this section. The adjusted explanatory power of all equations is acceptable. The explanatory power of the interactive regressions is superior to that of the noninteractive regressions.

The importance of household demand in influencing advertising intensity is evident, both as a separate variable in the noninteractive equations and as the interaction variable of equations 3 and 4 of each table. Both the nonconvenience good dummy and the durable dummy are negatively and significantly related to advertising intensity. The significance of the nonconvenience good dummy is superior in comparably specified equations. The overall explanatory power of the nonconvenience good equations is also superior.

Scientists and engineers as a fraction of total employment, used to reflect research and development activity, is usually significant and positively related in all equations. The hypothesis that new product introduction requires relatively greater advertising intensity is supported, as expected, most strongly in the interactive equations.

Table 4-2. Advertising Ordinary Least-Squares Regressions

Equation	1	2	3	4
Consumer Demand	0.037 (6.59)	0.034 (6.08)	*	*
Nonconvenience Good Dummy	−0.932E-2 (2.56)	−	−0.024 (5.43)	−
Durable Dummy	−	−0.826E-2 (1.54)	−	−0.034 (4.08)
Scientists & Engineers Fraction	0.076 (1.34)	0.084 (1.43)	1.122 (5.35)	1.454 (6.51)
C4 (3-digit)	0.115 (4.22)	0.122 (4.37)	0.036 (0.98)	−0.895E-2 (0.22)
(C4)² (3-digit)	−0.159 (4.57)	−0.165 (4.63)	−0.110 (1.83)	−0.021 (0.32)
Excess Profit/Sales	0.344 (6.84)	0.340 (6.56)	0.731 (6.35)	0.644 (5.30)
Constant	−0.024 (4.56)	−0.026 (4.77)	0.567E-2 (4.68)	0.483E-2 (3.75)
$\bar{R}^2$	0.601	0.576	0.823	0.801

Dependent variable: Advertising Intensity.

*These equations are interactive in Consumer Demand. All independent variables except the constant are multiplied by Consumer Demand prior to regression.

Number of observations: 71.

t-statistics shown in parentheses. Significance levels for a one-tailed $t(60)$ are:

> 0.10 : 1.30
> 0.05 : 1.67
> 0.01 : 2.39

However, the causality of this relationship may be questioned. Both R & D and advertising may result from the intrinsic differentiability of the industry's products. Causally, advertising results in part from intrinsic differentiability, which becomes realized differentiation through R & D.

The hypothesis of a nonlinear relation between advertising intensity and concentration is supported by the results of equations 1 and 2 of each table. The peak occurs in these equations between 0.36 and 0.37 for the 3-digit C4, whose average is 0.28, and between 0.61 and 0.63 for the weighted average 4-digit C4, whose average is 0.55.

The effect of profitability is shown in all equations. In unreported regressions, total before-tax profit divided by sales produced somewhat inferior results.[32]

Table 4-3. Advertising Ordinary Least-Squares Regressions

Equation	1	2	3	4
Consumer Demand	0.040 (6.32)	0.038 (6.12)	*	*
Nonconvenience Good Dummy	−0.909E-2 (2.17)	−	−0.027 (5.27)	−
Durable Dummy	−	−0.010 (1.79)	−	−0.035 (4.34)
Scientists & Engineers Fraction	0.084 (1.28)	0.088 (1.31)	1.196 (5.31)	1.389 (5.75)
C4 (4-digit)	0.116 (2.15)	0.143 (2.66)	0.019 (0.78)	−0.032 (1.40)
(C4)^2 (4-digit)	−0.095 (2.01)	−0.113 (2.40)	−0.069 (1.67)	0.018 (0.49)
Excess Profit/Sales	0.270 (4.89)	0.267 (4.78)	0.906 (7.08)	0.760 (5.86)
Constant	−0.039 (2.55)	−0.049 (3.18)	0.592E-2 (4.73)	0.549E-2 (4.18)
$\bar{R}^2$	0.506	0.495	0.825	0.807

Dependent variable: Advertising Intensity.

*These equations are interactive in Consumer Demand. All independent variables except the constant are multiplied by Consumer Demand prior to regression.

Number of observations: 71.

t-statistics shown in parentheses. Significance levels for a one-tailed $t(60)$ are:

$$0.10 : 1.30$$
$$0.05 : 1.67$$
$$0.01 : 2.39$$

Table 4-4 presents results of testing the joint influence of each of the noninteractive and interactive sets of independent variables in regressions that include both sets but which are not reported here. For equations utilizing the nonconvenience good dummy, the null hypothesis that the noninteractive variables do not add significant explanatory power cannot be rejected at the 0.10 level. For the durable dummy equations, this null hypothesis is rejected at the 0.05 or 0.01 level. The rejection may be due to the superior explanatory power of the noninteractive concentration variables in the durable dummy equations though no explanation for this pattern is apparent. The strong rejection of the null hypothesis that the interactive variables add no explanatory power is not surprising. The additional power of these variables includes the effect of consumer demand. On the basis either

Table 4-4.   Hypothesis Testing: Advertising

This table presents results of testing the joint influence of noninteractive and interactive variables in regression results not reported. The null hypothesis is that the set of variables, either noninteractive or interactive, jointly adds no explanatory power to equations containing both sets of variables and a constant. The specifications of equations on which these tests are based are equations 3 and 4 of Tables 4-2 and 4-3 to which the noninteractive variables Nonconvenience Good Dummy or Durable Dummy, Scientists & Engineers Fraction, C4, $(C4)^2$, and Excess Profit/Sales have been added.

F-statistics	*Noninteractive variables add no explanatory power to variables interactive with Consumer Demand*	*Variables interactive with Consumer Demand add no explanatory power to noninteractive variables*
C4 (3-digit): Nonconvenience		
Good Dummy	0.89	37.34
Durable Dummy	2.68	36.58
C4 (4-digit): Nonconvenience		
Good Dummy	0.68	45.23
Durable Dummy	3.54	51.28

Degrees of freedom are (5, 60).

Significance levels for $F(5, 60)$ are:

$$0.10 : 1.95$$
$$0.05 : 2.37$$
$$0.01 : 3.34$$

of adjusted explanatory power of equations in Tables 4-2 and 4-3 or formal hypothesis testing, the interactive specification is clearly superior.

In conclusion, this section has developed a model of the determinants of advertising intensity that receives strong support in empirical testing. Most advertising is directed to household consumers. Thus the principal determinant of advertising intensity is the proportion of industry sales going to household consumers. A number of additional influences are also demonstrated. The degree to which retailers influence product differentiation through their own sales efforts is an important influence, as is the relative propensity of the industry to develop new consumer products. The effect of producer competition on advertising intensity is demonstrated through the nonlinear relation between advertising intensity and concentration. The availability of profits to invest in advertising projects is also shown to be an influence.

DOMESTIC PRODUCER CONCENTRATION

Few manufacturing industries are thought of as perfectively competitive. Instead, industries are termed "monopolistically competitive" or "oligopolistic." We observe a continuum from very competitive industries to tight-knit oligopolies. A number of measures are developed to express this continuum. The four-firm concentration ratio (C4) is used here.

Although concentration is usually considered a part of market structure, it is hypothesized to be determined at least in part by barriers to entry, another aspect of market structure. Three domestic entry barriers are especially important and quantifiable.[33]

The first is based on technological considerations and is defined as the minimum efficient scale of plant relative to total market size. Minimum efficient scale (MES) is defined as the smallest output for which the long-run average cost per unit of output reaches a minimum. If MES/Market is relatively large, cost-minimizing efficiency dictates fewer producers and therefore a higher concentration ratio.

Related to this measure is the capital requirement for entry at minimum efficient scale. If much capital must be raised and invested to enter into production for a market, the riskiness of the entry is likely to raise the average cost of obtaining this investment capital and to put entrants at an absolute cost disadvantage relative to established firms. This inhibition to entry is associated with higher concentration, other things being equal.

Each of these technology variables acts as an entry barrier only if the cost disadvantage to smaller scale production is significant. Otherwise, entry at a scale smaller than MES does not put the entrant at a disadvantage relative to the existing firms.

Other absolute cost barriers, as patents or other production knowledge not freely disseminated, raw material source rights in vertically integrated industries, and the entrant's potential disadvantage in obtaining management personnel or other scarce factors of production, may also deter entry and tend to increase concentration. However, these determinants are not easily quantified.

A third significant barrier is advertising expenditure associated with product differentiation. Advertising by an entrant is a particularly risky investment in that the intangible asset created may have little if any salvage value. The entrant faces an absolute cost disadvantage because of the risk premium associated with borrowing necessary capital.[34] In addition, any scale economies in advertising penalize entry at small scale to avoid risking a larger investment. Although the evidence on media-pricing-based economies of scale is not decisive,[35] consumer thresholds for advertising messages per unit of time exist below which advertising effectiveness per message is decreased.[36] We expect that in industries in which advertising is an important part of the marketing effort, concentration is higher, other things being equal. Concentration can therefore be considered:

C4 = f (MES/Market, Capital Requirements, Cost-

disadvantage Ratio, Advertising Intensity)   (4-5)

The variables used in this estimation were discussed in Chapter 2 and are defined in Table A-1. Two measures of concentration are used as the dependent variable, one a weighted average of 4-digit C4 and the other C4 measured directly at the 3-digit level using IRS data. Because the 3-digit measure of C4 is not adjusted for geographic extent of market, either the adjusted number of markets in the United States or the 80 percent shipping radius, a measure of ease of transportability, is included as an additional determinant of 3-digit C4.[37]

Equation 4-5 is linearized for estimation. An alternative specification separates the ratio of MES to industry shipments from the adjusted number of markets and assumes interactions among the variables:

$$C4 = a \cdot \left(\frac{MES}{Shipments} \cdot NMARK\right)^{a_1} \cdot \left(\frac{MES}{Shipments} \cdot\right.$$

$$\left. TASS\right)^{a_2} \cdot (\text{Cost-disadvantage Ratio})^{a_3} \cdot (NMARK)^{a_4}$$

$$\cdot\, e^{a_5\,(\text{Advertising Intensity})}$$
                                                              (4-6)

where NMARK is the adjusted number of markets and TASS is industry total assets. The first variable in parentheses is MES/Market and the second is capital requirements. Advertising is entered exponentially because it can be zero. The coefficient a_4 is assumed to be zero for C4 (4-digit), which is adjusted for geographic extent of the market.

Equation 4-6 may be estimated in its natural log form:

$$Log(C4) = b + b_1\,Log(\text{MES/Shipments}) + b_2\,Log$$

$$(NMARK) + b_3\,Log(TASS) + b_4\,Log\,(\text{Cost-disadvantage}$$

$$\text{Ratio}) + b_5\,(\text{Advertising Intensity})$$
                                                              (4-7)

where

$$b_1 = a_1 + a_2 \qquad\qquad (4\text{-}8)$$

$$b_2 = a_1 + a_4 \qquad\qquad (4\text{-}9)$$

$$b_3 = a_2 \qquad\qquad (4\text{-}10)$$

$$b_4 = a_3 \qquad\qquad (4\text{-}11)$$

$$b_5 = a_5 \qquad\qquad (4\text{-}12)$$

If a_4 is assumed equal to zero, the other a_i coefficients are overidentified.

OLS estimates of the linear version of Equation 4-5 are presented in Table 4-5. OLS estimates of Equation 4-7 are presented in Table 4-6. In Table 4-6 results of estimation in which log (80 percent Shipping Radius) replaces log(NMARK) are also presented.

The results of linear estimation are generally consistent with our hypotheses but are not especially robust. Technological factors in part determine concentration. Capital requirements are robust between the measures of C4. The cost-disadvantage ratio is significant only in affecting C4 (3-digit). Advertising intensity is significant only in affecting C4 (4-digit).[38] The effect of geographic extent of the market on the understatement of C4 (3-digit) for regional industries is seen in the negative coefficient on adjusted number of markets and the positive coefficient on the 80 percent shipping radius, although the latter is insignificant.

The results of Table 4-6 are more robust across measures of C4. For C4 (3-digit), equation 1 indicates that a_1 equals 0.123 and a_4 equals −0.056. All a_i except the coefficient on advertising intensity have the expected signs. For C4 (4-digit), equation 3 indicates that a_1 equals either 0.005 or 0.079. The latter is the coefficient on adjusted number of markets, as a_4 is assumed to be zero. Perhaps Shepherd's adjustment of C4 for regional industries is overstated. All a_i coefficients are of the expected sign according to the results of equation 3.

Equations 2 and 4 of Table 4-6 utilize log (80 percent Shipping Radius) in place of log(NMARK). Other coefficients are similar. The explanatory power of the equations decreases slightly. The coefficient on the 80 percent shipping radius is negative, as expected, since the number of markets and the mile radius are inversely related.

This section has developed and tested hypotheses about the determinants of the long-run equilibrium level of concentration across manufacturing industries. Concentration, adjusted to reflect

Table 4-5. **Concentration Ordinary Least-Squares Regressions**

Equation	1	2	3
MES/Market	0.352	−0.081	0.493
	(1.14)	(0.40)	(3.29)
Capital Requirements	0.101E-3	0.106E-3	0.868E-4
	(5.67)	(5.64)	(5.82)
Cost-disadvantage Ratio	−0.360	−0.363	−0.074
	(1.79)	(1.76)	(0.43)
Advertising Intensity	−0.656	−0.493	1.501
	(0.67)	(0.49)	(1.80)
Adjusted Number of Markets	−0.196E-2	−	−
	(1.81)		
80% Shipping Radius	−	0.152E-4	−
		(0.27)	
Constant	0.570	0.555	0.528
	(2.92)	(2.68)	(3.18)
$\bar{R}^2$	0.395	0.365	0.430

Dependent variable: C4 (3-digit) in equations 1 and 2.
C4 (4-digit) in equation 3.

Number of observations: 71.

t-statistics shown in parentheses. Significance levels for a one-tailed $t(60)$ are:

0.10 : 1.30
0.05 : 1.67
0.01 : 2.39

geographic extent of the market, is affected by technologically based efficiency considerations, both the MES plant size relative to the size of the market and the capital requirements needed to establish such a plant. Concentration depends less consistently on the intensity of advertising by the industry.

SPECIFICATION OF STRUCTURAL MODELS

In previous chapters and sections of this chapter, the determinants of six aspects of industrial product markets in long-run equilibrium were developed. Before restating these equations as part of a full structural model, we discuss the choice of variables as endogenous or exogenous.

Firm conduct should, if possible, be endogenous. On this basis the profitability variables, representing pricing behavior, advertising intensity, export share, and FDI intensity are all endogenous variables. The only conduct variable not treated as endogenous is the research and development variable, scientists and engineers as a fraction of total employment. R & D intensity is considered exogenous, as there is

Table 4-6. Concentration Ordinary Least-Squares Regressions

Equation	1	2	3	4
MES/Shipments (Log)	0.441 (6.68)	0.425 (6.26)	0.176 (6.65)	0.181 (6.68)
Adjusted Number of Markets (Log)	0.067 (1.27)	−	0.079 (3.74)	−
80% Shipping Radius (Log)	−	−0.159E-2 (0.02)	−	−0.144 (3.56)
Total Assets (Log)	0.318 (4.18)	0.314 (4.07)	0.171 (5.60)	0.174 (5.65)
Cost-disadvantage Ratio (Log)	−0.413 (0.69)	−0.490 (0.80)	−0.205 (0.85)	−0.195 (0.80)
Advertising Intensity	−2.053 (0.55)	−2.128 (0.56)	1.044 (0.69)	0.809 (0.53)
Constant	−2.609 (2.94)	−2.615 (2.30)	−1.612 (4.53)	−0.640 (1.41)
$\bar{R}^2$	0.484	0.471	0.565	0.558

Dependent variable: C4 (3-digit) (Log) in equations 1 and 2.
C4 (4-digit) (Log) in equations 3 and 4.

Number of observations: 71.

t-statistics shown in parentheses. Significance levels for a one-tailed $t(60)$ are:

0.10 : 1.30
0.05 : 1.67
0.01 : 2.39

no empirically useful theory of its variance across industries. Any such theory requires as a central feature a measure of technological opportunity. No measure of this influence as it varies across industries could be constructed.

Two elements of market structure, concentration and import share, are considered sufficiently influenced by other structure and by conduct to be endogenous although concentration is discussed further at the end of this section.

All other variables used in the analysis are exogenous. Some of these, including MES/market, capital requirements, the capital-sales ratio, the capital-labor ratio, and average labor skill, represent the technology of the industry. Others, including the fraction of output sold to household consumers, natural resource requirements, transportability, and growth, are characteristics of the product. A third set of variables, including tariff rates, quotas, and other nontariff barriers to trade, are determined by the government.

The distinction between exogenous and endogenous variables is of course not absolute. It is partly one of degree and partly one based upon the goals of the book. Firms in an industry can influence technology, product characteristics, and government import policy, but their impact on these factors is less than their direct control over pricing, promotion, and foreign sales. In addition, because the book examines the influence of international trade on domestic prices and profits to derive policy implications, the government policy variables are considered exogenous and subject to unilateral change by the government. The goal of this book is not to examine the political determinants of policy, but rather to suggest that government policy toward imports has implications for market performance.

A model of structure and conduct in manufactured good product markets is now presented.[39] The model is based upon previous discussion of the determinants of each of the dependent variables.

$$\text{Profit/Sales} = a + a_1 \text{ (Capital/Sales)} + a_2 \text{(C4} \cdot \text{Cost-adjusted}$$
$$\text{MES/Market)} + a_3 \text{ (C4} \cdot \text{Cost-adjusted Capital Requirements)}$$
$$+ a_4 \text{ (C4} \cdot \text{Advertising Intensity)} + a_5 \text{ (C4} \cdot \text{Growth)} + a_6$$
$$\text{(C4} \cdot \text{Scientists \& Engineers Fraction)} + a_7 \text{ (C4} \cdot \text{Import Share)}$$
$$+ a_8 \text{ (C4} \cdot \text{Export Share)} + a_9 \text{ (C4} \cdot \text{Nominal Tariff Rate)}$$

$$(4\text{-}13)$$

$$\text{Import Share} = b + b_1 \text{ (Capital-Labor Ratio)} + b_2 \text{ (Skill}$$
$$\text{Index)} + b_3 \text{ (Natural Resource Dummy)} + b_4 \text{ (Scientists \&}$$
$$\text{Engineers Fraction)} + b_5 \text{ (80\% Shipping Radius)} + b_6$$
$$\text{(Advertising Intensity)} + b_7 \text{ (Before-tax Profit/Sales)} \qquad (4\text{-}14)$$

$$\text{Export Share} = c + c_1 \text{ (Capital-Labor Ratio)} + c_2 \text{ (Skill}$$
$$\text{Index)} + c_3 \text{ (Natural Resource Dummy)} + c_4 \text{ (Scientists \&}$$
$$\text{Engineers Fraction)} + c_5 \text{ (80\% Shipping Radius)} + c_6$$
$$\text{(Advertising Intensity)} \qquad (4\text{-}15)$$

$$\text{FDI Intensity} = d + d_1 \text{ (Advertising Intensity)} + d_2$$
$$\text{(Scientists \& Engineers Fraction)} + d_3 \text{ (Managers Fraction)}$$
$$+ d_4 \text{ (Natural Resource Dummy)} + d_5 \text{ (C4)} + d_6 \text{ (Cost-}$$
$$\text{adjusted Capital Requirements)} \qquad (4\text{-}16)$$

Advertising Intensity $= e + e_1$ (CD · Nonconvenience

Good Dummy) $+ e_2$ (CD · Scientists & Engineers

Fraction) $+ e_3$ (CD · C4) $+ e_4$ (CD · $[C4]^2$) $+ e_5$

(CD · Excess Profit/Sales) $\qquad$ (4-17)

$Log(C4) = f + f_1$ Log(MES/Shipments) $+ f_2$ Log(80%

Shipping Radius) $+ f_3$ Log(Total Assets) $+ f_4$ Log

(Cost-disadvantage Ratio) $+ f_5$ (Advertising Intensity), $\quad$ (4-18)

where CD is Consumer Demand.

An alternative specification of the profitability equation utilizes $1/[1\text{-log}(C4)]$ as the interaction variable:

Profit/Sales $= g + g_1$ (Capital/Sales) $+ g_2$ (Z · Cost-

adjusted MES/Market) $+ g_3$ (Z · Cost-adjusted Capital

Requirements) $+ g_4$ (Z · Advertising Intensity) $+ g_5$

(Z · Growth) $+ g_6$ (Z · Scientists & Engineers Fraction)

$+ g_7$ (Z · Import Share) $+ g_8$ (Z · Export Share) $+ g_9$

(Z · Nominal Tariff Rate) $\qquad$ (4-19)

where

$$Z = 1/[1 - \log (C4)] \qquad (4\text{-}20)$$

The other government policy variables, the quota and NTB variables, are not included in the model, nor is the nominal tariff rate included in the import share equation. Their inclusion adds little to the explanatory power of the model. Their inclusion would cause serious multicollinearity in the import share equation, as noted in Chapter 3.

Previous discussion suggests one important substantive question regarding these models: should concentration be considered exogenous or endogenous? In the third section a number of determinants of C4 were discussed. Many other determinants, both additional entry bar-riers and historical circumstances in particular industries, are not easi-ly quantified. The efficiency of simultaneous estimation may be adversely affected because much information is lost by using the pre-dicted rather than the actual levels of concentration. Other discussion suggests that it is the actual rather than the predicted level of concentration that is relevant. In the profitability equation, concentration is entered interactively because it represents the degree to which mutual interdependence is likely to constrain competitive behavior. This effect is a function of the actual (observed) level of concentration rather than the predicted level. Both of these arguments suggest that concentration should be considered exogenous. Therefore, the model is estimated with C4 both exogenous, a five-equation structural model, and endogenous, a six-equation structural model.

ESTIMATION TECHNIQUE

A number of estimation techniques are available to estimate systems of equations. Consideration is given to two-stage least squares (TSLS), limited information maximum likelihood (LIML), three-stage least squares (3SLS), and full-information maximum likelihood (FIML).[40] The asymptotic properties of these estimators are known.[41] TSLS and LIML are consistent and asymptotically efficient, given the amount of information utilized.[42] The asymptotic efficiency of 3SLS and FIML is superior because both of them utilize information about restrictions on all equations in the system. FIML and 3SLS are consistent and asymptotically efficient, achieving the Cramer-Rao bound.[43] All of these assertions assume that the system is correctly specified. If misspecification is present, Fisher has shown that asymptotically neither TSLS nor LIML is generally preferable.[44]

Much less is known about the small sample properties of these estimators. Some mathematical work has been done on general properties of special cases, but most knowledge is based on so-called Monte Carlo studies, which attempt to establish small sample properties empirically. These studies are not unanimous in their conclusions. In general, differences among the techniques are small.[45] TSLS tends to be the best simultaneous method, according to root mean square error (RMSE), in the presence of multicollinearity among the exogenous variables, misspecification, or both.[46] Indeed, TSLS is desirable in the presence of misspecification because it tends to isolate the misspecification within individual equations, while both 3SLS and FIML spread the specification error throughout the system.[47] These properties suggest that TSLS is more robust than any other of the simultaneous techniques.

Because misspecification and multicollinearity are likely to be present in the models and data used, TSLS is chosen as the technique to estimate each of the simultaneous systems. An important property of TSLS necessary to the study is that it is an instrumental variables estimation technique. The variables considered as endogenous right-hand side variables need not be determined by an exact specification elsewhere in the system. Rather TSLS requires only that a set of exogenous variables produces estimated or fitted values of the endogenous variable. The set of fitted values is used as an instrument for the endogenous variable in the second stage of estimation. As an instrumental variables estimator, TSLS retains the asymptotic property of consistency in the presence of this sort of system misspecification.

Estimates of each equation utilizing OLS were presented. OLS produces estimates that are likely biased in the sample and asymptotically inconsistent.[48] The inconsistency is a result of included endogenous right-hand side variables that are correlated with the equation's error term, violating one assumption of the classical regression model.[49] In Monte Carlo studies, OLS tends to be more biased in the sample than any of the simultaneous techniques.[50] At the same time, however, OLS estimates tend to have the least variance.[51] If point estimates are desired, OLS is potentially superior to TSLS or any other method, according to a loss function such as root mean square error. Monte Carlo studies suggest that no one method tends to be superior on the basis of RMSE.[52] However, Monte Carlo studies do show that inference using OLS estimates tends to be poor due to the OLS bias.[53] Inference should rather be done with consistent estimates such as those produced by TSLS.[54]

RESULTS OF ESTIMATION OF THE STRUCTURAL MODEL

Results of estimation of the model assuming C4 is exogenous are presented in Table 4-7 and 4-8 for C4 (3-digit) and C4 (4-digit), respectively. Results of estimation of the model assuming C4 is endogenous are presented in Tables 4-9 and 4-10. These latter tables actually form a whole as the instrument list is the same in each table. The alternate form of the profitability equation, Equation 4-19, is not presented in Tables 4-7 and 4-8. In each of these estimations, the number of degrees of freedom is forty-six or greater. This is generally considered large enough to approach the large sample property of consistency of TSLS.

Instrumental variables used in the estimation are given in each of the tables. The list of instrumental variables is not exhaustive. In Tables 4-7 and 4-8 the list of instruments should probably include each individual variable plus each individual variable (except consumer demand as a fraction of total output and C4) multiplied by consumer demand as a fraction of total output, C4, and the product of these two interaction variables. This would produce a list of instruments whose number is larger than the number of observations, making estimation

Table 4-7.   Two-Stage Least-Squares Estimation

Dependent Variable	$\dfrac{Profit}{Sales}$*	Import Share	Export Share	FDI Intensity	Advertising Intensity*
Equation	1	2	3	4	5
Capital/Sales	0.029 (3.85)	—	—	—	—
Cost-adjusted MES/Market	0.221 (2.12)	—	—	—	—
Cost-adjusted Capital Requirements	0.426E-5 (1.10)	—	—	-0.166E-4 (0.83)	—
Advertising Intensity	1.164 (3.60)	-0.374 (1.12)	-0.559 (2.09)	1.734 (2.41)	—
Growth	0.042 (1.16)	—	—	—	—
Scientists & Engineers Fraction	-0.281 (1.29)	0.018 (0.07)	0.712 (3.37)	1.427 (3.37)	1.098 (4.13)
Import Share	-0.241 (1.88)	—	—	—	—
Export Share	0.276 (1.50)	—	—	—	—
Nominal Tariff Rate	0.107 (1.42)	—	—	—	—
Capital-Labor Ratio	—	0.401E-3 (0.98)	0.287E-3 (0.83)	—	—
Skill Index	—	-0.520E-4 (2.13)	0.371E-4 (1.86)	—	—
Natural Resource Dummy	—	0.035 (1.07)	-0.024 (0.86)	0.188 (2.59)	—
80% Shipping Radius	—	0.257E-4 (1.69)	0.341E-4 (2.69)	—	—

Before-Tax Profit/Sales	—	—	—	0.299 (1.42)	—
Managers Fraction	—	1.335 (2.00)	—	—	—
C4 (3-digit)	0.032 (0.67)	0.218 (2.87)	—	—	—
(C4)² (3-digit)	-0.105 (1.51)	—	—	—	—
Nonconvenience Good Dummy	-0.024 (5.26)	—	—	—	—
Excess Profit/Sales	0.754 (3.89)	—	—	—	—
Constant	0.567E-2 (4.67)	-0.076 (1.76)	-0.239 (1.82)	0.338 (2.15)	0.012 (2.15)
SSR	0.397E-2	0.609	0.084	0.111	0.688E-2
SSR (OLS)	0.397E-2	0.606	0.083	0.106	0.686E-2

*These equations are interactive. See Equations 4-13 and 4-17.

Instrumental variables: Capital/Sales, Cost-adjusted MES/Market, (C4 · Cost-adjusted MES/Market), Cost-adjusted Capital Requirements, (C4 · Cost-adjusted Capital Requirements), Growth, (C4 · Growth), Scientists & Engineers Fraction. (C4 · Scientists & Engineers Fraction), (CD · Scientists & Engineers Fraction), Nominal Tariff Rate, (C4 · Nominal Tariff Rate), Capital-Labor Ratio, Skill Index, Natural Resource Dummy, 80% Shipping Radius, Managers Fraction, C4, (CD · C4), (C4)², (CD · [C4]²), Nonconvenience Good Dummy, (CD · Nonconvenience Good Dummy), CD; where C4 is C4 (3-digit) and CD is Consumer Demand.

Number of Observations: 71.

Asymptotic *t*-statistics shown in parentheses. Significance levels for a one-tailed test are

0.10 : 1.28
0.05 : 1.65
0.01 : 2.33

Table 4-8.   Two-Stage Least-Squares Estimation

Dependent Variable	Profit/Sales*	Import Share	Export Share	FDI Intensity	Advertising Intensity*
Equation	1	2	3	4	5
Capital/Sales	0.037 (4.47)	—	—	—	—
Cost-adjusted MES/Market	0.035 (1.95)	—	—	—	—
Cost-adjusted Capital Requirements	0.992E-5 (3.30)	—	—	-0.251E-6 (0.01)	—
Advertising Intensity	0.421 (3.36)	-0.331 (0.96)	-0.610 (2.22)	1.447 (1.86)	—
Growth	0.055 (2.86)	—	—	—	—
Scientists & Engineers Fraction	-0.184 (1.43)	0.023 (0.10)	0.714 (3.37)	1.415 (3.03)	1.172 (4.78)
Import Share	-0.065 (0.66)	—	—	—	—
Export Share	0.057 (0.49)	—	—	—	—
Nominal Tariff Rate	0.130 (2.88)	—	—	—	—
Capital-Labor Ratio	—	0.525E-3 (1.32)	0.310E-3 (0.89)	—	—
Skill Index	—	-0.439E-4 (1.83)	0.368E-4 (1.84)	—	—
Natural Resource Dummy	—	0.029 (0.91)	-0.025 (0.90)	0.179 (2.33)	—
80% Shipping Radius	—	0.300E-4 (2.01)	0.340E-4 (2.67)	—	—

	(1)	(2)	(3)	(4)	(5)
Before-Tax Profit Sales	—	0.066 (0.32)	—	—	—
Managers Fraction	—	—	—	1.175 (1.69)	—
C4 (4-digit)	—	—	—	0.174 (1.88)	0.018 (0.73)
C4² (4-digit)	—	—	—	—	-0.071 (1.68)
Nonconvenience Good Dummy	—	—	—	—	-0.027 (5.08)
Excess Profit/Sales	—	—	—	—	0.944 (4.75)
Constant	-0.326E-3 (0.05)	0.296 (1.92)	-0.236 (1.80)	-0.099 (1.81)	0.593E-2 (4.73)
SSR	0.752E-2	0.106	0.084	0.648	0.404E-2
SSR (OLS)	0.719E-2	0.106	0.083	0.644	0.403E-2

*These equations are interactive. See Equations 4-13 and 4-17.

Instrumental variables: The same variables as in Table 4-7, but C4 is C4 (4-digit).

Number of observations: 71.

Asymptotic t-statistics shown in parentheses. Significance levels for a one-tailed are:

0.10 : 1.28
0.05 : 1.65
0.01 : 2.33

Table 4-9. Two-Stage Least-Squares Estimation

| Dependent Variable | Profit/Sales* | | | | Import Share | Export Share |
| | Interactive with C4 (3-digit) | | Interactive with C4 (4-digit) | | | |
Equation	1	2	3	4	5	6
Capital/Sales	0.040 (3.54)	0.040 (3.98)	0.038 (4.05)	0.040 (4.33)	—	—
Cost-adjusted MES/Market	0.176 (1.50)	0.088 (1.95)	0.035 (1.92)	0.038 (2.08)	—	—
Cost-adjusted Capital Requirements	0.896E-5 (1.47)	0.895E-5 (2.02)	0.102E-4 (2.87)	0.999E-5 (2.99)	—	—
Advertising Intensity	1.261 (3.00)	0.802 (3.81)	0.482 (3.65)	0.498 (4.06)	-0.438 (1.21)	-0.697 (2.56)
Growth	0.040 (0.85)	0.041 (1.52)	0.043 (2.07)	0.036 (2.02)	—	—
Scientists & Engineers Fraction	-0.297 (0.98)	-0.216 (1.08)	-0.269 (1.81)	-0.231 (1.67)	-0.070 (0.27)	0.622 (2.86)
Import Share	-0.394 (1.40)	-0.214 (1.09)	-0.123 (0.74)	-0.103 (0.69)	—	—
Export Share	0.185 (0.69)	0.144 (0.84)	0.158 (1.19)	0.161 (1.31)	—	—
Nominal Tariff Rate	0.079 (0.79)	0.096 (1.50)	0.113 (2.13)	0.099 (2.15)	—	—

Capital-Labor Ratio	—	—	—	—	0.339E-3 (0.82)	0.323E-3 (0.94)
Skill Index	—	—	—	—	-0.482E-4 (1.84)	0.460E-4 (2.24)
Natural Resource Dummy	—	—	—	—	0.035 (1.07)	-0.029 (1.06)
80% Shipping Radius (Log)	—	—	—	—	0.017 (1.94)	0.023 (3.12)
Before-tax Profit / Sales	—	—	—	—	0.423 (1.60)	—
Constant	0.824E-2 (1.13)	0.305E-2 (0.47)	0.732E-2 (0.12)	-0.264E-2 (0.40)	0.218 (1.13)	-0.414 (2.66)
SSR	0.811E-2	0.730E-2	0.739E-2	0.754E-2	0.114	0.082

*These equations are interactive. The specification of equations 1 and 3 is Equation 4-13. The specification of equations 2 and 4 is Equation 4-19.

Instrumental Variables: Capital/Sales, Cost-adjusted MES/Market, Cost-adjusted Capital Requirements, Growth, Scientists & Engineers Fraction, (CD · Scientists & Engineers Fraction), Nominal Tariff Rate, Capital-Labor Ratio, Skill Index, Natural Resource Dummy, 80% Shipping Radius (Log), Managers Fraction, (CD · Nonconvenience Good Dummy), CD, MES/Shipments (Log), Total Assets (Log), Cost-disadvantage Ratio (Log); where CD is Consumer Demand.

Number of observations: 71.

Asymptotic t-statistics shown in parentheses. Significance levels for a one-tailed test are:

0.10 : 1.28
0.05 : 1.65
0.01 : 2.33

Table 4-10.   Two-Stage Least-Squares Estimation

Dependent Variable	FDI Intensity		Advertising Intensity*		C4 (3-digit) (Log)	C4 (4-digit) (Log)
Equation	1	2	3	4	5	6
Cost-adjusted Capital Requirements	-0.222E-4 (1.03)	-0.121E-5 (0.06)	—	—	—	—
Advertising Intensity	1.716 (2.28)	1.741 (2.18)	—	—	-0.749 (0.18)	0.789 (0.46)
Scientists & Engineers Fraction	1.346 (3.05)	1.402 (2.77)	1.123 (3.74)	1.119 (3.25)	—	—
Natural Resource Dummy	0.182 (2.49)	0.180 (2.28)	—	—	—	—
80% Shipping Radius (Log)	—	—	—	—	-0.592E-3 (0.01)	-0.144 (3.56)
Managers Fraction	1.342 (1.99)	1.077 (1.54)	—	—	—	—
C4 (3-digit)	0.263 (2.59)	—	0.038 (0.59)	—	—	—
(C4)² (3-digit)	—	—	-0.079 (0.92)	—	—	—
C4 (4-digit)	—	0.177 (1.43)	—	0.023 (0.60)	—	—
(C4)² (4-digit)	—	—	—	-0.117 (1.91)	—	—

	(1)	(2)	(3)	(4)	(5)	(6)
Nonconvenience Good Dummy	—	—	-0.024 (4.94)	-0.031 (5.28)	—	—
Excess Profit/Sales	—	—	0.668 (2.53)	1.222 (4.61)	—	—
MES/Shipments (Log)	—	—	—	—	0.418 (6.10)	0.181 (6.63)
Total Assets (Log)	—	—	—	—	0.315 (4.08)	0.174 (5.65)
Cost-disadvantage Ratio (Log)	—	—	—	—	-0.442 (0.72)	-0.196 (0.80)
Constant	-0.085 (1.87)	-0.099 (1.56)	0.562E-2 (4.52)	0.601E-2 (4.55)	-2.685 (2.35)	-0.639 (1.40)
SSR	0.612	0.654	0.408E-2	0.446E-2	19.760	3.154

*These equations are interactive. See Equation 4-17.

Instrumental variables: The same variables as in Table 4-9.

Number of observations: 71.

Asymptotic t-statistics shown in parentheses. Significance levels for a one-tailed test are:

0.10 : 1.28
0.05 : 1.65
0.01 : 2.33

impossible. The problem would be worse if C4 is endogenous (Tables 4-9 and 4-10). Fortunately, since TSLS is an instrumental variables method, the asymptotic property of consistency applies even if only a subset of all reasonable instrumental variables is utilized in estimation, although the actual sample efficiency of the estimation is likely reduced.[55]

The TSLS results are generally very similar to OLS results presented previously. However, the bias of OLS coefficients is apparent in a number of instances.

Import penetration is hypothesized to reduce domestic firms' profitability, other things being equal. Pricing over cost is hypothesized to act as an additional incentive to imports, other things being equal. The former effect was established by OLS estimation in Chapter 2. The latter could not be demonstrated in Chapter 3 using OLS. The incentive effect of domestic pricing on import penetration is demonstrated using TSLS. The coefficient on before-tax profit per dollar of sales is positive in Tables 4-7, 4-8, and 4-9. It is significant in Tables 4-7 and 4-9.

A related variable, (before-tax) excess profit per dollar of sales, is positive though insignificant if substituted for before-tax profit per dollar of sales in these equations. Apparently, some foreign firms treat exports to the United States as marginal sales that need not cover the opportunity cost of capital used in production.

The coefficients on advertising intensity are also biased in OLS estimation. The coefficients are larger and more significant in the TSLS estimation of the import share, export share, and FDI equations. The standard errors of advertising in the profitability equation and of excess profit in the advertising equation increase although the coefficients vary only slightly. These coefficients remain significant at the 0.01 level.

In the profitability equations the coefficient on import share is larger in TSLS estimation although its standard error increases more than proportionally. The coefficient on the nominal tariff rate is smaller in TSLS. In general TSLS produces a decrease in the significance of the coefficients in the profitability equations.

In Table 4-9 four specifications of the profitability equation are estimated by TSLS. The explanatory power is poor only for equation 1 although all of the variables except capital/sales in each of these equations are instrumented by their fitted values because the interaction variable is endogenous. Equations 2 and 4 use $1/[1 - \log C4]$ as the interaction variable.

Approximate tests of the null hypothesis that the three international trade variables add no significant explanatory power to the profitability equations are computed.[56] Only equation 1 of Table 4-9 fails to reject the null hyhpothesis. The other equations reject the null hypothesis at the 0.05 or 0.01 level.

CONCLUSIONS

A number of related structural models of product markets in long-run equilibrium were estimated.[57] Two methodological conclusions are suggested by the estimation results. Two-stage least squares is a reasonable method for analyzing a full system of industrial organization relationships in that the loss of efficiency relative to OLS is small. The results indicate that ordinary least-squares estimates are not seriously biased for nearly all of the relations explored here. These observations imply that the conclusions of previous work on estimation of individual equations using OLS are not necessarily invalid although inference using OLS may be inappropriate. On the other hand, there is the implication that TSLS is a viable estimation technique for industrial organization research whose use should be expanded, especially as most of this research is directed to hypothesis testing rather than point estimation.

In particular cases OLS may produce seriously biased results. Thus only unbiased TSLS estimation demonstrates the effect of pricing and profitability on import penetration. In addition, the effect of advertising intensity as a barrier to trade is more effectively demonstrated in TSLS.

Appendix 4-1
FDI Data

Data on FDI activity are not plentiful at the 3-digit level of industry classification. The best measure of the outward FDI intensity of an industry would be a measure of the importance of foreign direct investment activity to total industry activity. The two most likely candidates, the fraction of total assets in FDI entities or the fraction of total sales accounted for by FDI operations, are not available at this level of aggregation.[58] Therefore, FDI intensity is measured as the fraction of total after-tax equity profits that are identifiable foreign subsidiary and branch profits as reported in the *IRS Sourcebook Statistics of Income Corporations*. Total equity profits are profits after-tax net of the domestic investment tax credit. Identifiable foreign profits are branch foreign tax credits[59] plus repatriated foreign subsidiary profits after foreign tax (foreign dividends received) plus foreign tax credits on these repatriated foreign subsidiary profits.[60] In symbols,

$$F = t_B \pi_B + p(1 - t_s) \, \pi_s + p t_s \pi_s$$
$$= t_B \pi_B + p \pi_S \tag{4-21}$$

where F is identifiable foreign profit, π is before-tax equity profit, t is the tax rate, p is the dividend payout rate on after-tax subsidiary earnings, the subscript B refers to branch operations, and the subscript s refers to subsidiary operations.[61] Profit before tax is understated for both branches and subsidiaries. For branches only foreign tax credits can be identified. For subsidiaries only their repatriated earnings (but not their retained earnings) can be identified. In the aggregate, p and t_B are similar, each being about 0.4.[62] The degree of understatement for branches and subisdiaries is likely similar. In addition, branch activity is only a small fraction of subsidiary activity,[63] and thus any difference in the degree of understatement is not likely important. However, the dividend payout rate p may vary across industries, creating unknown biases in the measure.

The measure of total equity profit P used here is approximately[64]

$$P = (1 - t_D)\ (\pi_D + \pi_B + p\pi_B) \tag{4-22}$$

where the subscript D refers to U.S. variables. This measure understates total after-tax profitability by omitting foreign subsidiary retained earnings.

The measure of FDI activity as a fraction of total activity is

$$\frac{F}{P} = \frac{t_B \pi_B + p\pi_s}{(1 - t_D)(\pi_D + \pi_B + p\pi_s)} \tag{4-23}$$

If t_B, p, and t_D are approximately equal, as they are in the aggregate,[65] the fraction is approximately

$$\frac{F}{P} \approx \frac{t_D}{(1 - t_D)}\ \frac{\pi_B + \pi_s}{\pi_D + \pi_B + p\pi_s} \tag{4-24}$$

This measure tends to overstate the importance of FDI activity as subsidiary retained earnings are not included in the denominator of the second fraction, but to understate the importance as $t_D < 0.5$ and therefore $t_D/(1 - t_D) < 1$. In addition, variations in p, t_B, and t_D across industries bias the ratio as a cross-industry measure in empirically unknown ways. The measure nonetheless is a direct measure of the fraction of total industry activity attributable to FDI operations.

The reporting of FDI profits and assets is also important in relation to the variables profit/sales and capital/sales. This measure of profit includes all identifiable foreign profit. The capital measure includes the book value of the parents' equity in both foreign subsidiaries and foreign branches. In notation, total after-tax profit TP as measured in profit/sales is equal to:

$$TP = (1 - t_D)\ (\pi_D + \pi_B + p\pi_s) + I_D \tag{4-25}$$

where I_D is interest paid on the debt of the parent. Total capital TC as measured in capital/sales is equal to:

$$TC = E_D + A_D + E_B + E_s \qquad (4\text{-}26)$$

where E refers to equity participation and A refers to assets financed by debt rather than equity.

For foreign branches the reporting of profits matches the reporting of assets, so there is no systematic bias. However, for foreign subsidiaries, only after-tax repatriated foreign profits are reported, due to deferral of foreign-source income taxation. Relative to foreign subsidiary assets as reported, foreign subsidiary profits are understated. A downward bias is created in the profit-capital relationships. In addition, any variations in the relative rates of profit between domestic and foreign operations or in dividend payout rates across industries create unknown statistical biases.

NOTES

1. In 1970, branch earnings were 2.4 percent of total earnings of U.S. foreign direct investment in manufacturing. U.S. Department of Commerce, *Survey of Current Business*, November 1972, pp. 21-26.

2. For U.S. manufacturing as a whole, book value at year end of inward FDI was 17 percent (1966) and 19 percent (1970) of outward FDI. U.S. Department of Commerce, *Survey of Current Business*, February 1972, pp. 29-33, and September 1973, pp. 20-25.

3. C.F. Bergsten, T. Horst, and T. Moran, *American Multinationals and American Interests*, 1978, partially summarized in T. Horst, "American Multinationals and the U.S. Economy," *American Economic Review*, May 1976.

4. S. Hymer, *International Operations of National Firms: A Study of Direct Foreign Investments*, 1976.

5. R.E. Caves, "International Corporations: The Industrial Economics of Foreign Investment," *Economica*, February 1971.

6. Caves.

7. Discussed in R.E. Caves, "Causes of Direct Investment: Foreign Firms Shares in Canadian and United Kingdom Manufacturing Industries," *Review of Economics and Statistics*, August 1974.

8. F.T. Knickerbocker, *Oligopolistic Reaction and Multinational Enterprise*, 1973.

9. Caves, "International Corporations: The Industrial Economics of Foreign Investment," p. 10.

10. This concept is illuminated in K.J. Arrow, "Vertical Integration and

Communication," *Bell Journal of Economics*, Spring 1975.

11. J.S. Bain, *Barriers to New Competition*, 1956, pp. 144-156.

12. R. Vernon, "International Investment and International Trade in the Product Cycle," *Quarterly Journal of Economics*, May 1966.

13. T. Horst, "The Industrial Composition of U.S. Exports and Subsidiary Sales to the Canadian Market," *American Economic Review*, March 1972.

14. Bergsten, Horst, and Moran, partially summarized in T. Horst, "American Multinationals and the U.S. Economy."

15. An interactive effect between C4 and the natural resource dummy has been suggested in that only concentrated industries can preclude entry although cause and effect are commingled. Because our two natural resource industries have nearly equal concentration, this interaction can be safely ignored.

16. Caves, "Causes of Direct Investment: Foreign Firms Shares in Canadian and United Kingdom Manufacturing Industries."

17. T. Horst, "Firm and Industry Determinants of the Decision to Invest Abroad: An Empirical Study," *Review of Economics and Statistics*, August 1972.

18. Caves, "Causes of Direct Investment: Foreign Firms Shares in Canadian and United Kingdom Manufacturing Industries.

19. Horst, "The Industrial Composition of U.S. Exports and Subsidiary Sales to the Canadian Market," and Horst, "Firm and Industry Determinants of the Decision to Invest Abroad: An Empirical Study.

20. Caves, "Causes of Direct Investment: Foreign Firms Shares in Canadian and United Kingdom Manufacturing Industries."

21. Most previous studies used large firms' percentage of total industry sales rather than concentration. These two measures tend to be collinear. Concentration was used here because the dependent variable already excludes firms with assets less than $500,000.

22. Horst, "Firm and Industry Determinants of the Decision to Invest Abroad: An Empirical Study."

23. In addition, the measure of FDI intensity was added to export share regressions reported in Chapter 3, Table 3-4. Collinearity of determinants also appears to have overwhelmed the hypothesized tradeoff between exporting and FDI.

24. Knickerbocker, *Oligopolistic Reaction and Multinational Enterprise*, 1973. His theory hypothesized and found empirical support for a nonlinear relation between product market concentration and his entry concentration index. This nonlinear relation is not hypothesized for the overall level of FDI activity, and no support could be found here for the significance of a squared C4 term empirically.

25. R.E. Caves, *International Trade, International Investment, and Imperfect Markets*, 1974.

26. A.D. Strickland and L.W. Weiss, "Advertising, Concentration, and Price-Cost Margins," *Journal of Political Economy*, October 1976, used a durable dummy in developing an advertising model similar to the one developed here.

27. M.E. Porter, "Consumer Behavior, Retailer Power, and Market Performance in Consumer Goods Industries," *Review of Economics and*

Statistics, February 1974, and M.E. Porter, *Interbrand Choice, Strategy, and Bilateral Market Power*, 1976.

28. D.F. Greer, "Advertising and Market Concentration," *Southern Economic Journal*, July 1971.

29. J. Backman, *Advertising and Competition*, 1967, chs. 2 and 3, stresses this aspect.

30. W.S. Comanor and T.P. Wilson, *Advertising and Market Power*, 1974, ch. 7.

31. Some studies have attempted to avoid the interactive effects by estimating only across "consumer goods" industries. This approach is rejected here because the data indicate that there is not a dichotomy between producer good and consumer good industries but a continuum.

32. Comanor and Wilson, pp. 143-163, find support for either total (not excess) profit or cash flow (each as a fraction of sales) as a determinant of advertising in a simultaneous system.

33. J.S. Bain, *Barriers to New Competition*, and "Theory Concerning the Condition of Entry" in *Essays on Price Theory and Industrial Organization*, 1972.

34. Comanor and Wilson, ch. 4.

35. Comanor and Wilson, pp. 53-61.

36. Comanor and Wilson, pp. 49-53.

37. L.W. Weiss, "The Geographic Size of Markets in Manufacturing," *Review of Economics and Statistics*, August 1972.

38. M.E. Porter, "Consumer Behavior, Retailer Power, and Market Performance in Consumer Goods Industries," finds that advertising affects concentration only in consumer convenience goods industries. A variable having values equal to the advertising intensity for consumer convenience goods industries and zero otherwise was substituted for advertising intensity in each equation reported in Tables 4-5 and 4-6. The performance of this new formulation declined for both the advertising coefficient and overall explanatory power.

39. A recent study, Strickland and Weiss, develops and estimates a structural model that does not include international aspects.

40. These methods are discussed in H. Theil, *Principles of Econometrics*, ch. 10, and in J. Johnston, *Econometric Methods*, second edition, ch. 13.

41. The following discussion applies to overidentified systems. Each equation in each of our models is overidentified. If all other equations are exactly identified in the system, estimates for the equation under consideration will be equal in the sample for TSLS and 3SLS on the one hand and LIML and FIML on the other. J. Kmenta, *Elements of Econometrics*, pp. 577, 581-582.

42. Theil, pp. 497, 504-507, and C.F. Christ, *Econometric Models and Methods*, p. 465.

43. Theil, p. 536.

44. F.M. Fisher, "The Relative Sensitivity of Specification Error of Different k-Class Estimators," *Journal of the American Statistical Association*, 1966, discussed in Johnston, p. 393.

45. Johnston, p. 417.

46. Johnston, pp. 412-413, 419-420.

47. Theil, pp. 428-429.

48. Christ, p. 453-465.

49. Kmenta, pp. 348, 380.

50. Johnston, p. 410.

51. Johnston, p. 412.

52. Johnston, pp. 412-413.

53. Johnston, pp. 413-414.

54. Johnston, p. 414.

55. Christ, p. 446, states that TSLS is a way of "averaging" too much information that arises if one tries to apply an instrumental variables approach to an overidentified equation.

56. The statistic $N \cdot$ Log (SSR_R/SSR_U) is distributed approximately χ^2 (q), where N is the number of observations. SSR the sum of squared residuals, R the restricted equation, U the unrestricted, and q the number of imposed restrictions. Based on reported unrestricted equations and unreported TSLS estimation of restricted equations,

Table	Equation	$\chi^2(3)$
4-7	1	16.41
4-8	1	8.30
4-9	1	3.73
4-9	2	9.55
4-9	3	13.59
4-9	4	13.77

Significance levels for $\chi^2(3)$ are 6.25, 7.81, and 11.30 for the 0.10, 0.05, and 0.01 levels, respectively. The statistics are approximate because TSLS does not minimize the SSR in the sample.

57. Attempts to isolate the relations between FDI and export share or import share produce insignificant TSLS results.

58. N.K. Bruck and F.A. Lees, *Foreign Investment, Capital Controls, and the Balance of Payments,* 1968, develop a measure of the foreign content of consolidated operations based upon assets or sales Fortune 500 firms and aggregated to the 3-digit SIC level. For those industries that could be matched, their measure correlates closely with the measure used here.

59. U.S. tax laws allow a tax credit for foreign taxes deemed paid on foreign earnings up to the amount of the tentative U.S. tax liability on these earnings.

60. Only repatriated earnings are taxable in the United States because of U.S. deferral of taxation until foreign income is returned to this country. The combination of deferral, the foreign tax credit, and the ability to use an overall method in computing the tentative U.S. tax liability and tax credit (rather than a per country method) results in the United States collecting little tax on manufacturing FDI operations.

61. This analysis abstracts from certain other features of U.S. taxation of foreign source income as the lack of gross-up of dividends from LDCs before computation of tentative U.S. taxes and the treatment of nondividend repatriation of funds.

62. T. Horst, "American Taxation of Multinational Firms," *American Economic Review,* June 1977.

63. In 1970, branch earnings were 2.4 percent of total earnings of U.S. foreign direct investment in manufacturing. U.S. Department of Commerce, *Survey of Current Business,* November 1972, pp. 21-26.

64. As with foreign source income, the analysis of U.S. taxation abstracts from certain aspects of domestic taxation such as loss provisions and the investment tax credit.

65. Horst, "American Taxation of Multinational Firms." His use of the statutory U.S. tax rate overstates the effective U.S. tax rate.

✳   *Chapter 5*

Policy Implications

Certain policy implications follow from the results presented in the preceding chapters. To the extent that import competition constrains pricing in relatively concentrated industries, allocative efficiency may be improved by opening these industries to increased import competition. In addition, increased protection offered to these industries to maintain and to expand domestic employment need not result in increased domestic output and employment. The results also offer insight into the debate about antitrust action based on a shared monopoly or tacit collusion hypothesis. Allocative efficiency may be improved by deconcentration through antitrust action even if barriers to entry cannot be lowered. This chapter examines each of these implications and concludes by identifying those who are likely to gain and likely to lose if policies designed to improve allocative efficiency are implemented. The chapter does not attempt any comparison of these distributional and efficiency effects, however, as this is beyond the goals and resources of this book.

IMPORT COMPETITION

Results reported in Chapters 2 and 4 demonstrate that import competition constrains pricing in relatively concentrated industries. Foreign firms inject additional competition into the domestic market. To improve allocative efficiency the government should set its import policy in these industries to allow maximum foreign competitive influence, by reducing tariffs, eliminating and avoiding quotas, and lowering other nontariff barriers to trade.

These results offer insight into current efforts to increase protection against imports. Support for increased protection is often based on its relation to increased domestic employment. The results presented here suggest that increased protection offered to relatively concentrated industries is likely to produce a domestic price effect that reduces, and perhaps completely substitutes for, the domestic output and employment effects.

The employment and price effects of an increase in the tariff rate may be explored theoretically in a model of a domestic monopolist facing import competition. Let marginal cost MC, import supply Q_M, and domestic demand Q_D be as shown in Figure 5-1. The increase in the tariff, assuming it does not become prohibitive, shifts import supply to Q'_M and changes the residual demand curve ABQ_D to EFQ_D. Marginal revenue shifts from MR to MR'. Domestic price increases from p to p'. Domestic output increases from Q_p to Q'_p. Increased protection increases output and employment, but the increase in price reduces the output effect. If price had not risen, output would have increased to Q''_p. The effect of protection on output is reduced because of the increase in domestic price.

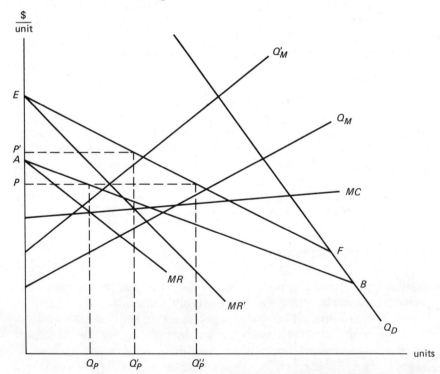

Figure 5-1. Tariff Increase and the Monopolist

This result may be generalized somewhat using a model similar to one developed in Chapter 2. For the monopolistic market, let

$$Q_D = f(p), \quad f' < 0 \tag{5-1}$$

$$Q_M = g(p_F) = g(\frac{p}{1+t}), \quad g' > 0 \tag{5-2}$$

$$MC = c \tag{5-3}$$

where p is domestic price, p_F is foreign received price, and t is the tariff rate. Foreign received price differs from domestic price according to the height of the tariff, ignoring transport costs:

$$p = (1 + t)p_F \tag{5-4}$$

Equilibrium for the monopolist occurs in a profit-maximizing position:

$$\text{Max } p \cdot Q_p - c \cdot Q_p \tag{5-5}$$

or

$$p + \frac{f - g}{f' - g' \ \dfrac{1}{1+t}} = c, \tag{5-6}$$

where Q_p is domestic output.

Let the elasticity of domestic demand be ϵ_D and of import supply be ϵ_M:

$$\epsilon_D = -p \frac{f'}{f} \tag{5-7}$$

and

$$\epsilon_M = p_F \frac{g'}{g} = \frac{p}{1+t} \frac{g'}{g} \tag{5-8}$$

These elasticities are assumed constant. The optimum price can be written as

$$p = \frac{c(f\epsilon_D + g\epsilon_M)}{f(\epsilon_D - 1) + g(\epsilon_M + 1)} \tag{5-9}$$

Manipulation of Equation 5-9 yields

$$\frac{dp}{dt} = \frac{c(g' \frac{p}{(1+t)^2} f[\epsilon_M + \epsilon_D])}{(f[\epsilon_D - 1] + g[\epsilon_M + 1])^2 - c(f'g - g'f\frac{1}{(1+t)})(\epsilon_D + \epsilon_M)}$$

(5-10)

which is greater than zero. Price rises with an increase in the tariff rate. The change in domestic output with an increase in the tariff rate is

$$\frac{d(Q_D - Q_M)}{dt} = (f' - g'\frac{1}{(1+t)})\frac{dp}{dt} + g'\frac{p}{(1+t)^2}$$

(5-11)

which is in general indeterminate. Q_D will fall due to the rise in p. Q_M may fall by a greater or lesser amount, and thus domestic output may increase or decrease. Finger has shown that the indeterminate output effect holds in the general case of nonlinear domestic demand and import-supply functions facing a monopolist.[1]

Organized labor in the United States has recently been requesting import quotas to restrain import competition. Their goal is to maintain and to expand domestic employment. Theoretical analysis demonstrates that the imposition of a quota to protect a domestic import-competing monopolist results in nonmarginal changes in domestic output and price.[2] Domestic output falls and domestic price rises in response to the imposition of a quota that reduces only slightly the actual level of imports. Only a relatively restrictive quota results in an increase in domestic output. Indeed, under certain reasonable circumstances, domestic output falls with the imposition of any binding quota.

Figure 5-2 demonstrates the effects of quota imposition on a domestic monopolist. The initial level of imports is Q_{MF}. The imposition of a quota reduces imports by k to Q_{MQ}. MR shifts to MR'. The domestic monopolist maintains output at Q_P and raises price to p_Q from p_F. If quota imposition reduces the import level by a greater amount, domestic output rises. If the quota imposition reduces imports by a lesser amount, domestic output falls.

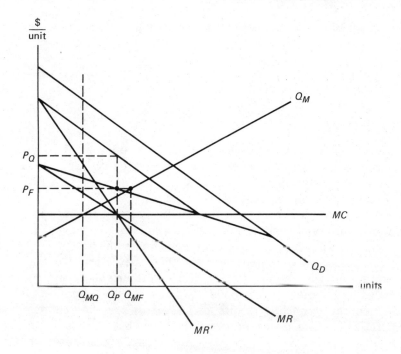

Figure 5-2. Quota Imposition and the Monopolist

Linear forms of Equations 5-1 and 5-2 can be used to show that, given the tariff rate,[3]

$$dQ_p \overset{\geq}{\underset{<}{=}} 0 \text{ as } k \overset{\geq}{\underset{<}{=}} - \frac{\frac{g'}{1+t} Q_p}{(f' - \frac{g'}{1+t})} \tag{5-12}$$

Domestic output increases only if the import reduction k due to quota imposition is relatively large. No quota level, even zero, results in an increase in domestic production if

$$Q_{MF} < - \frac{\frac{g'}{1+t} Q_p}{(f' - \frac{g'}{1+t})} \tag{5-13}$$

The effect of quota imposition on domestic price is

$$dp = \frac{\dfrac{g'}{1+t}Q_p - (f' - \dfrac{g'}{1+t})k}{2f'\,(f' - \dfrac{g'}{1+t})} \tag{5-14}$$

Thus domestic price increase is a positive function of the restrictiveness of the imposed quota. In addition, a quota that reduces the import level only slightly, in that k is small, results in a relatively large, nonmarginal increase in domestic price.

Finger has also shown that, if domestic demand and import supply functions are nonlinear, a reduction in the level of an existing quota results in an indeterminate effect on the monopolist's output.[4] These results taken as a whole indicate that theoretically there is no presumption that domestic output rises if increased protection is granted to a domestic monopolist.

Given the empirical results presented in previous chapters, the theoretical results may apply to industries that exhibit oligopolistic market imperfections. As we have shown that concentrated domestic oligolopies tend to approach the joint profit maximizing or monopolistic pricing outcome, the theoretical results suggest that increased protection offered to relatively concentrated industries leads to an increase in price not related to increased cost. Expected increases in domestic output and employment will be reduced, and perhaps eliminated, by the reduction in total domestic demand resulting from the price increase.

ANTITRUST

Results reported in Chapters 2 and 4 lend empirical support to oligopoly theories that predict that increasing producer concentration tends to allow increasing realization of a joint profit maximizing outcome based on recognized mutual interdependence and tacit collusion.[5] These results also demonstrate that this collusive ability affects pricing in an interactive manner with barriers to entry and other aspects of market structure and conduct. The results present statistical support for antitrust action based on a shared monopoly hypothesis. Even if entry barriers cannot be reduced, reduction of concentration is likely to improve allocative efficiency by making tacit collusion more difficult.

There are a number of objections and qualifications to this conclusion. A major objection is that the data used to obtain the statistical results are imperfect.[6] However, this study replicates the findings of many other studies for different data sources, years, and even countries.[7] This is the first study to test the interactive hypothesis using a continuous relationship and regression analysis. Statistical support for the interactive hypothesis strengthens the argument in favor of antitrust action.

A qualification of the argument for antitrust is that technical efficiency should not be impaired, that is, unit cost should not rise as a result of deconcentration. Concentration levels exceed those required for the achievement of MES by the major firms in many industries.[8] Knowledge of multiplant economies is much less precise, but for most industries they appear to be minimal.[9] If firms become large only because of superior efficiency, any move to deconcentrate would sacrifice these firm efficiencies.[10] However, the relatively secure position of large firms in concentrated industries reduces the necessity for cost minimization. These large firms become relatively inefficient because the pressure of competition in imposing cost minimization is absent. Examples may be cited to support each of these positions. No definitive conclusion is possible given the present state of knowledge.

Another qualification of the argument for antitrust is that technological progressiveness should not be reduced.[11] The secure position and cash flow of large firms in concentrated industries may permit risky, large-scale research and development activity. Nonetheless, competitive pressure may assure the development and application of new knowledge. A middle ground, though not a consensus, is found in the argument that the best market structure for technological progressiveness is that of a moderately concentrated industry.[12] Larger firms with the ability to undertake large-scale innovation are present. Smaller firms form an important competitive fringe to speed innovation and diffusion. In addition, basic inventive concepts may originate in these smaller firms. Again, however, no definitive conclusion can be reached about these competing hypotheses given our current state of knowledge.

These objections and qualifications indicate that it is best to continue antitrust policy on a basis of case by case or industry by industry. It is hoped that the decision to prosecute is based upon proper consideration of admittedly uncertain potential benefits and costs. Given the difficulty of demonstrating tacit collusion as an aspect of market conduct, antitrust law may require revision to allow greater weight to be placed upon the number and size distribution of sellers within a market.

DISTRIBUTIONAL ASPECTS OF IMPROVING ALLOCATIVE EFFICIENCY

Improvement in allocative efficiency is beneficial to the economy as a whole in that improvement would allow more value to be created with a given set of factor inputs. Increasing import competition and antitrust aimed at deconcentration are each likely to improve allocative efficiency in relatively concentrated industries. The distributional consequences of these policies may also be important.

The major gainers in a movement toward greater allocative efficiency are consumers. Prices are lowered and output expanded. If imports increase the range of products available, consumers may also benefit from the increased variety within their choice set.

Major losers in the movement toward greater allocative efficiency are likely to be present stockholders of the affected firms. Most of these stockholders are innocent of any relation to monopolistic practices in that their financial investments earn only a normal rate of return. Monopoly profit has been capitalized into the value of the stocks. A movement toward greater allocative efficiency tends to create capital losses for these present stockholders as the current and future profitability of the corporation is reduced.

Another possible loser is labor. If labor is able to appropriate some of excess return available due to product market power, a lessening of this power tends to depress the earnings of labor in these industries.[13] Labor is also a loser if employment in affected industries drops, which is likely if import competition increases. Workers in specific industries thus may be adversely affected. Some transitional costs are cushioned by unemployment insurance and trade adjustment assistance. Other workers tend to benefit in their role as consumers.

NOTES

1. J.M. Finger, "Protection and Domestic Output," *Journal of International Economics*, November 1971.

2. For analysis additional to that presented here, see T.A. Pugel, "Quota Imposition, Output, and Monopoly," New York University Faculty of Business Administration Working Paper No. 78-83.

3. For further results, see T. Ophir, "The Interaction of Tariffs and Quotas," *American Economic Review*, December 1969. Certain of his results depend on the existence of a quota level that exceeds the initial import level and thus is initially nonbinding.

4. Finger.

5. For a summary of these theories, see L.W. Weiss, "The Concentration-Profits Relationship and Antitrust," in H.J. Goldschmid, H.M. Mann, and J.F. Weston, eds., *Industrial Concentration: The New Learning*, 1974.

6. For instance, we have used accounting rates of return that may not reflect actual economic profitability. The concentration variables are imperfect in measurement and may not accurately reflect the actual state of domestic producer competition. The concordances used to integrate various data sources are also imperfect.

7. L.W. Weiss.

8. J.M. Blair, *Economic Concentration*, 1972, ch. 5.

9. J.S. Bain, *Barriers to New Competition*, 1956, ch. 2, and F.M. Scherer et al., *The Economics of Multi-Plant Operations*, 1975, chs. 5 to 7.

10. H. Demsetz, "Two Systems of Belief About Monopoly," in Goldschmid, Mann, and Weston.

11. For a survey of theory and empirical results in this area, see J.W. Markham, "Concentration: A Stimulus or Retardant to Innovation?", in Goldschmid, Mann, and Weston.

12. F.M. Scherer, "Market Structure and the Employment of Scientists and Engineers," *American Economic Review*, June 1967. This proposition is further discussed in R.E. Caves, *American Industry: Structure, Conduct, Performance*, fourth edition, 1977, ch. 5.

13. See T.A. Pugel, "Profitability, Concentration, and the Interindustry Variation in Wages," New York University Faculty of Business Administration Working Paper No. 78-84; C.T. Haworth and C.J. Reuther, "Industrial Concentration and Interindustry Wage Determination," *Review of Economics and Statistics*, February 1978; and L.W. Weiss, "Concentration and Labor Earnings," *American Economic Review*, March 1966.

Appendix Tables

Table A-1: Variable Definitions and Sources

Variable	Definition and Source
Advertising Intensity (0.016, 0.019)	Advertising purchased (1967-1970) divided by business receipts (1967-1970) [*IRS Sourcebook Statistics of Income Corporations* 1967-1970].
Adjusted Number of Markets (8.620, 28.817)	The number of markets in the continental United States is calculated from the 80% Shipping Radius according to Weiss's cutoff points. A local industry is given the value of 144. This number is then adjusted to be equal to one if the number is four or less and to be equal to itself if the number is five or more.
Before-Tax Profit Sales (0.079, 0.034)	Before-Tax Profit (including state and local interest received) plus Interest paid on debt divided by Business Receipts (each summed over 1967-1970) [*IRS Sourcebook Statistics of Income Corporations,* 1967-1970], for firms with assets exceeding $500,000 each.
C4 (3-digit) (0.283, 0.186)	Four-firm concentration ratio, 1967, measured directly at the 3-digit level by dividing the business receipts of the four largest firms (according to total assets) by the business receipts of all firms in the industry [*IRS Sourcebook Statistics of Income Corporations,* 1967].
C4 (4-digit) (0.553, 0.163)	Four-firm concentration ratio, 1966, obtained as a weighted average of adjusted 4-digit concentration ratios [Shepherd, *Market Power and Economic Welfare*], weights being the shipments of the 4-digit industries comprising the 3-digit industry. Shepherd's concentration ratios were adjusted for geographic and product market definition but where Sheperd's geographic market extent did not agree with Weiss's, [Weiss, "The Geographic Size of Markets in Manufacturing," *Review of Economic and Statistics,* August 1972], an attempt to readjust was made.
Capital-Labor Ratio (26.042, 14.493)	Total Assets net of depreciation divided by Business Receipts (each summed over 1967-1970) [*IRS Sourcebook Statistics of Income Corporations* 1967-1970] multiplied by the ratio of Shipments to Total Employment (each summed over 1967-1970) [U.S. Bureau of Census, *Census of Manufactures,* 1967 and *Annual Survey of Manufactures,* 1968-1970]
Capital Requirements (572, 1009)	Total Assets multiplied by MES/Shipments. The variable is measured in hundreds of thousands of dollars.
Capital/Sales (0.785, 0.211)	Total assets net of depreciation (1967-1970) divided by business receipts (1967-1970) [*IRS Sourcebook Statistics of Income,* 1967-1970], for firms with assets exceeding $500,000 each.
Consumer Demand (0.247, 0.293)	Household Consumer Demand divided by Total Output, 1967 [U.S. Bureau of Economic Analysis, *Input-Output Structure of the U.S. Economy,* 1967. Vol. I].
Cost-adjusted Capital Requirements (204, 673)	The Cost-disadvantage Ratio is used to adjust Capital Requirements as follows: If the ratio is greater than 0.90, Cost-adjusted Capital Requirements equals zero. If the ratio is 0.90 or less, Cost-adjusted Capital Requirements is equal to Capital Requirements.

Table A-1 continued

Variable	Definition and Source
Cost-adjusted MES/Market (0.022, 0.097)	The Cost-disadvantage Ratio is used to adjust MES/Market as follows: If the ratio is greater than 0.90, Cost-adjusted MES/Market equals zero. If the ratio is 0.90 or less, Cost-adjusted MES/Market is equal to MES/Market.
Cost-disadvantage Ratio (0.918, 0.095)	Value added per worker in smaller plants producing one half of industry output (excluding plants with ten or fewer workers) divided by value added per worker in larger plants producing the other one half of industry output [U.S. Bureau of the Census, *Census of Manufactures*, 1967].
Durable Dummy (0.099, 0.298)	Dummy variable equal to one if the industry is considered to sell primarily consumer durables. [U.S. Bureau of the Census, *Census of Population, 1970*] is the basic source according to their durable-nondurable classification of industries (see Table A-2 for industries considered to sell primarily consumer durables).
Effective Tariff Rate (0.182, 0.179)	Average of 1964 and 1972 effective tariff rates. [Baldwin, *Nontariff Distortions of International trade*]. These rates include nontariff barriers in their calculation. The concordance between Baldwin's industries and the IRS industries is rather poor.
80% Shipping Radius (777, 372)	The mile radius within which 80 percent of industry shipments were made [U.S. Bureau of the Census *Census of Transportation Commodity Transportation Survey,* Vol. III, 1963], calculated according to the method suggested by Weiss [Weiss, "The Geographic Size of Markets in Manufacturing," *Review of Economics and Statistics,* August 1972]. Certain industries considered to face centralized demand (IRS 2228, 2250, 2298, and 2830) were assigned a mile radius of 1,100. As no data were published on the printing and publishing industries, Newspapers (2711) and Other Printing and Publishing (2798) were considered to be local industries given a mile radius of 68, and Periodicals (2712) and Books, Greeting Cards, and Miscellaneous Publishing (2715) were considered to be national industries given a mile radius of 1,100.
Excess Profit/ Sales (0.048, 0.032)	Before-tax Profit/Sales minus 0.04 times Capital/Sales.
Export Share (0.051, 0.049)	Exports divided by Shipments (each summed over 1967-1970) [U.S. Bureau of the Census, *U.S. Commodity Exports and Imports as Related to Output,* 1967-1970].
FDI Intensity (0.138, 0.125)	FDI Activity divided by Total Activity, represented by identifiable foreign profits divided by total after-tax profits, and calculated as Foreign Dividends plus Foreign Tax Credits divided by Net Profit After Tax plus State and Local Interest Received, each summed over 1967-1970 for firms with assets of $500,000 or more [*IRS Sourcebook Statistics of Income Corporations*] 1967-1970.
Import Share (0.046, 0.043)	Imports divided by Shipments minus Exports plus Imports (each summed over 1967-1970) [U.S. Bureau of the Census, *Commodity Exports and Imports as Related to Output,* 1967-1970].

Table A-1 continued

Variable	Definition and Source
Intra-Industry Trade (Supply Deflated) (0.048, 0.041)	Twice the lesser of Exports or Imports divided by Shipments plus Imports (each summed over 1967-1970) [U.S. Bureau of the Census, *Commodity Exports and Imports as Related to Output, 1967-1970*].
Intra-Industry Trade (Trade Deflated) (0.525, 0.268)	Twice the lesser of Exports or Imports divided by Exports plus Imports (each summed over 1967-1970) [U.S. Bureau of the Census, *Commodity Exports and Imports as Related to Output, 1967-1970*].
Managers Fraction (0.059, 0.019)	The proportion of Managers and Kindred Workers in Total Employment, 1969 [U.S. Bureau of the Census, *Census of Population, 1970, Subject Report 7C*].
Median Years of Schooling (11.797, 0.728)	Years of formal education, obtained as a weighted average of the male and female median years of formal education completed, weights being the share of each sex in total employment [U.S. Bureau of the Census, *Census of Population, 1970, Subject Report 7B*].
MES/Market (0.037, 0.101)	MES/Shipments multiplied by Adjusted Number of Markets.
MES/Shipments (0.010, 0.015)	MES is measured at the 4-digit level as the average size of the largest plants producing half of the industry's output in 1967. MES at the 3-digit level is obtained as a shipments-weighted average of constituent 4-digit MES and divided by total 1967 shipments for the 3-digit industry [U.S. Bureau of the Census, *Census of Manufactures, 1967*].
Natural Resource Dummy (0.028, 0.165)	Dummy with value of one for steel (IRS 3310) and nonferrous metals (IRS 3330).
Net Trade Position (Supply Deflated) (0.477E-2, 0.064)	Exports minus Imports all divided by Shipments plus Imports (each summed over 1967-1970) [U.S. Bureau of the Census, *U.S. Commodity Exports and Imports as Related to Output, 1967-1970*].
Net Trade Position (Trade Deflated) (0.035, 0.544)	Exports minus Imports all divided by Exports plus Imports (each summed over 1967-1970) [U.S. Bureau of the Census, *U.S. Commodity Exports and Imports as Related to Output, 1967-1970*].
Nominal Tariff Rate (0.101, 0.072)	Duties Collected divided by Imports (each summed over 1967-1970) [U.S. Bureau of the Census, *U.S. Commodity Exports and Imports as Related to Output, 1967-1970*].
Non-Convenience Good Dummy (0.239, 0.427)	Dummy variable equal to one if the industry is considered to sell primarily consumer nonconvenience goods. Porter's classification is the basic source (see Table A-2 for industries considered to sell primarily consumer nonconvenience goods). [Porter, "Consumer Behavior, Retailer Power, and Market Performance in Consumer Goods Industries," *Review of Economics and Statistics*, November 1974].
NTB (0.300, 0.357)	The percentage of Imports affected by nontariff barriers to trade, 1967 [Walter, "Non-Tariff Protection Among Industrial Countries: Some Preliminary Evidence," *Economia Internazionale*, May 1972]. The concordance between Walter's SITC industries and the IRS industries is rather poor.

Table A-1 continued

Variable	Definition and Source
Profit/Sales (0.047, 0.018)	Net after-tax profits (including state and local interest received) plus interest paid on debt (1967-1970) divided by business receipts (1967-1970) [*IRS Sourcebook Statistics of Income Corporations*, 1967-1970], for firms with assets exceeding $500,000 each.
Quota (0.113, 0.316)	Dummy with value one for apparel and textile industries (IRS 2228, 2250, 2298, 2310, 2330, 2380, 2398) and dairy products (IRS 2020). Based on Mintz survey [Mintz, *U.S. Import Quotas: Costs and Consequences*].
Scientists & Engineers Fraction (0.030, 0.029)	The proportion of Life and Physical Scientists and Engineers in Total Employment, 1969 [U.S. Bureau of the Census, *Census of Population, 1970, Subject Report 7C*].
Skill Index (6572, 291)	Median occupational earnings for each of seven occupation classes (PTK, Managers, Clerical, Sales, Craftsmen and Foremen, Operatives, Laborers) are obtained as a weighted average of male and female medians for these occupations, 1969. The Skill Index is then obtained as a weighted average of these, weights being the respective shares of each occupation group in total industry employment [U.S. Bureau of the Census, *1970 Census of Population, Subject Reports 7A and 7C*].
Total Assets (62325, 72355)	Total Assets net of depreciation, averaged over 1967-1970. [*IRS Sourcebook Statistics of Income Corporations*, 1967-1970]. In hundreds of thousands of dollars.

Notes: The numbers in parentheses below the variable name are the mean and standard deviation of the variable.

The entries in brackets in the variable definition are the data sources.

Table A-2: Consumer Nonconvenience Good Industries and Consumer Durable Industries

Consumer Nonconvenience Good Industries	*Consumer Durable Industries*
Knitting Mills (2250)	Household Furniture (2510)
Men's and Boy's Clothing (2310)	Household Appliances (3630)
Women's, Children's, Infants' Clothing (2330)	Radio, Television, and Communication Equipment (3660)
Miscellaneous Apparel and Accessories (2380)	Motor Vehicles and Equipment (3710)
Miscellaneous Fabricated Textile Products (2398)	Transportation Equipment nec (3798)
Household Furniture (2510)	Photographic Equipment (3860)
Rubber Products (3010)	Watches and Clocks (3870)
Footwear, Except Rubber (3140)	
Leather and Leather Products nec (3198)	
Cutlery, Hand Tools, and Hardware (3420)	
Household Appliances (3630)	
Radio, Television, and Communication Equipment (3660)	
Motor Vehicles and Equipment (3710)	
Transportation Equipment nec (3798)	
Optical, Medical, and Ophthalmic Goods (3830)	
Photographic Equipment (3860)	
Watches and Clocks (3870)	

Table A-3: Concordance Among IRS Minor Industries, Standard Industrial Classification (SIC), and Census of Population Detailed Industries.

IRS	SIC	Census of Population
2010	201	Meat products
2020	202	Dairy products
2030	203	Canning and preserving
2040	204	Grain-mill products
2050	205	Bakery products
2082	2082 + 2083	Beverage industries
2084	2084 + 2085	Beverage industries
2086	2086 + 2087	Beverage industries
2098	207 + 209	Miscellaneous food preparations and confectionary
2100	21	Tobacco manufactures
2228	221 + 222 + 223 + 226	Dyeing and finishing textiles and yarn, thread and fabric mills
2250	225	Knitting mills
2298	224 + 227 + 228 + 229	Miscellaneous textiles and yarn, thread and fabric mills, and floor coverings
2310	231 + 232	Apparel and accessories
2330	233 + 234 + 236	Apparel and accessories
2380	235 + 237 + 238	Apparel and accessories
2398	239	Miscellaneous fabricated textile products
2410	241 + 242	Logging and sawmills, planing mills, and millwork
2430	243	Sawmills, planing mills, and millwork
2498	244 + 249	Miscellaneous wood products
2510	251	Furniture and fixtures
2590	252 + 253 + 254 + 259	Furniture and fixtures
2620	261 + 262 + 263 + 266	Pulp, paper, and paperboard mills
2698	264 + 265	Paperboard containers and miscellaneous paper and pulp products
2711	271	Newspaper publishing and printing

Table A-3 continued

IRS	SIC	Census of Population
2712	272	Printing, publishing, and allied industries
2715	273 + 277 + 274	Printing, publishing, and allied industries
2798	275 + 276 + 278 + 279	Printing, publishing, and allied industries
2810	281 + 282	Industrial chemicals and plastics, synthetics and resins, and synthetic fibers
2830	283	Drugs and medicines
2840	284	Soaps and cosmetics
2850	285	Paints, varnishes, and related products
2898	286 + 287 + 289	Agricultural chemicals and miscellaneous chemicals and chemicals not specified
2998	295 + 299	Miscellaneous petroleum and coal products
3010	301 + 302 + 303 + 306	Rubber products
3098	307	Miscellaneous plastic products
3140	314	Footwear, except rubber
3198	311 + 312 + 313 + 315 + 316 + 317 + 319	Tanned, cured, and finished leather and leather products
3210	321 + 322 + 323	Glass and glass products
3240	324	Cement, concrete, gypsum, and plaster products
3270	327	Cement, concrete, gypsum, and plaster products
3298	325 + 326 + 328 + 329	Structural clay products and pottery and miscellaneous nonmetallic mineral products
3310	331 + 332 + 3391	Blast furnaces, steelworks, rolling mills, and other primary iron and steel industries
3330	333 + 334 + 335 + 336 + 3392 + 3399	Primary aluminum and other primary nonferrous industries
3410	341	Miscellaneous fabricated and not specified metal products
3420	342	Cutlery, handtools, and other hardware
3430	343	Miscellaneous fabricated and not specified metal products
3440	344	Fabricated structural metal products
3450	345	Screw machine products

3461	346	Metal stamping
3498	347 + 348 + 349	Miscellaneous fabricated and not specified metal products
3520	352	Farm machinery and equipment
3530	353	Construction and material handling machines
3540	354	Metalworking machinery
3550	355	Other machinery and not specified machinery
3560	356	Other machinery and not specified machinery
3570	357	Office and accounting machines and electronic computing
3580	358	Other machinery and not specified machinery
3598	351 + 359	Other machinery and not specified machinery and engines and turbines
3630	363	Household appliances
3660	365 + 366	Radio, television, and communication equipment
3662	367	Electrical machinery and not specified electrical machinery
3698	361 + 362 + 364 + 369	Electrical machinery and not specified electrical machinery
3710	371	Motor vehicles and motor vehicle equipment
3720	372	Aircraft and parts
3730	373	Ship and boat building and repairing
3798	374 + 375 + 379	Railroad equipment and mobile homes and cycles and miscellaneous transport
3810	381 + 382	Scientific and controlling instruments
3830	383 + 384 + 385	Optical and health services supplies
3860	386	Photographic equipment and supplies
3870	387	Watches, clocks, and clockwork-operated devices

Bibliography

Arrow, Kenneth J. "Vertical Integration and Communication," *Bell Journal of Economics* 6, 1 (Spring 1975).

Backman, Jules. *Advertising and Competition.* New York: New York University Press, 1967.

Bain Joe S. *Essays on Price Theory and Industrial Organization.* Boston: Little, Brown and Company, 1972.

———. *Barriers to New Competition.* Cambridge, Mass.: Harvard University Press, 1956.

Baldwin, Robert E. *Nontariff Distortions of International Trade.* Washington, D.C.: The Brookings Institution, 1970.

Ball, David Stafford. "United States Effective Tariffs and Labor's Share." *Journal of Political Economy* 84, 2 (April 1976).

Baumann, Harry. "Structural Characteristics of Canada's Trade Pattern." *Canadian Journal of Economics* 9, 3 (August 1976).

Becker, Gary S. *Human Capital,* second edition. New York: Columbia University Press, 1975.

Bergsten, C. Fred, Thomas Horst, and Thomas Moran. *American Multinationals and American Interests.* Washington, D.C.: The Brookings Institution, 1978.

Blair, John M. *The Control of Oil.* New York: Pantheon Books, 1976.

———. *Economic Concentration.* New York: Harcourt Brace Jovanovich, 1972.

Bloch, Harry. "Prices, Costs, and Profits in Canadian Manufacturing: The Influence of Tariffs and Concentration." *Canadian Journal of Economics* 7, 4 (November 1974).

Boyle, Stanley E. "The Average Concentration Ratio: An Inappropriate Measure of Industry Structure." *Journal of Political Economy* 81, 2 (March-April 1973).

Branson, William H. "U.S. Comparative Advantage: Some Further Results." *Brookings Papers on Economic Activity* no. 3, 1971.

––––––, and Helen B. Junz. "Trends in U.S. Trade and Comparative Advantage." *Brookings Papers on Economic Activity* 2, 1971.

Bruck, Nicholas K., and Francis A. Lees. *Foreign Investment, Capital Controls, and the Balance of Payments.* New York: New York University Graduate School of Business Administration, Institute of Finance, 1968.

Caves, Richard. *American Industry: Structure, Conduct, Performance,* fourth edition. Englewood Cliffs, N.J.: Prentice-Hall, 1977.

––––––. "Causes of Direct Investment: Foreign Firms' Shares in Canadian and United Kingdom Manufacturing Industries." *Review of Economics and Statistics* 56, 3 (August 1974).

––––––. *International Trade, International Investment, and Imperfect Markets.* Special Papers in International Economics No. 10. Princeton: International Finance Section, Department of Economics, Princeton University, 1974.

––––––. "International Corporations: The Industrial Economics of Foreign Investment." *Economica* 38, 149 (February 1971).

––––––, Javad Khalilzadeh-Shirazi, and Michael E. Porter. "Scale Economies in Statistical Analyses of Market Power." *Review of Economics and Statistics* 57, 2 (May 1975).

Cheh, John H. "A Note on Tariffs, Non-Tariff Barriers, and Labor Protection in the United States Manufacturing Industries." *Journal of Political Economy* 84, 2 (April 1976).

Christ, Carl F. *Econometric Models and Methods.* New York: John Wiley and Sons, 1966.

Cohen, Kalman J., and Richard M. Cyert. *Theory of the Firm: Resource Allocation in a Market Economy.* Englewood Cliffs, N.J.: Prentice-Hall, 1965.

Comanor, William S., and Thomas A. Wilson. *Advertising and Market Power.* Cambridge, Mass.: Harvard University Press, 1974.

Dam, Kenneth W. "Implementation of Import Quotas: The Case of Oil." *Journal of Law and Economics* 14, 1 (April 1971).

Eastman, H.C., and S. Stykolt. *The Tariff and Competition in Canada.* New York: St. Martin's Press, 1967.

Economic Report of the President, January 1977. Washington, D.C.: U.S. Government Printing Office, 1977.

Esposito, Louis, and Frances F. Esposito. "Foreign Competition and Domestic Industry Profitability." *Review of Economics and Statistics* 53, 4 (November 1971).

Finger, J.M. "Protection and Domestic Output." *Journal of International Economics* 1, 4 (November 1971).

Gale, Bradley T. "Market Share and Rate of Return." *Review of Economics and Statistics* 54, 4 (November 1972).

Gerber, David J. "The United States Sugar Quota Program: A Study in the Direct Congressional Control of Imports." *Journal of Law and Economics* 19, 1 (April 1976).

Goldschmidt, Harvey J., H. Michael Mann, and J. Fred Weston. *Industrial Concentration: The New Learning.* Boston: Little, Brown and Company, 1974.

Greer, Douglas F. "Advertising and Market Concentration." *Southern Economic Journal* 38, 1 (July 1971).

Grubel, Herbert G. "Intra-Industry Specialization and the Pattern of Trade." *Canadian Journal of Economics and Political Science* 33, 3 (August 1967).

_____, and P.J. Lloyd. *Intra-Industry Trade.* London: The MacMillan Press, 1975.

Gruber, William, Dileep Mehta, and Raymond Vernon. "The R & D Factor in International Trade and International Investment of United States Industries." *Journal of Political Economy* 75, 1 (February 1967).

Haworth, Charles T., and Carol Jean Reuther. "Industrial Concentration and Interindustry Wage Determination." *Review of Economics and Statistics* 60, 1 (February 1978).

Heckscher, Eli. "The Effect of Foreign Trade on the Distribution of Income." *Ekonomisk Tidskrift* 21 (1919).

Horst, Thomas. "American Taxation of Multinational Firms." *American Economic Review* 67, 3 (June 1977).

_____. *Income Taxation and Competitiveness in the United States, West Germany, France, the United Kingdom, and Japan.* Washington, D.C.: National Planning Association, 1977.

_____. "American Multinationals and the U.S. Economy." *American Economic Review* 66, 2 (May 1976).

_____. "Firm and Industry Determinants of the Decision to Invest Abroad: An Empirical Study." *Review of Economics and Statistics* 54, 3 (August 1972).

_____. "The Industrial Composition of U.S. Exports and Subsidiary Sales to the Canadian Market." *American Economic Review* 62, 1 (March 1972).

Hufbauer, Gary C. "The Taxation of Export Profits." *National Tax Journal* 28, 1 (March 1975).

Hurdle, Gloria J. "Leverage, Risk, Market Structure and Profitability." *Review of Economics and Statistics* 56, 4 (November 1974).

Hymer, Stephen. *International Operations of National Firms: A Study of Direct Foreign Investments.* Cambridge, Mass.: M.I.T. Press, 1976.

International Economic Report of the President. January 1977. Washington, D.C.: U.S. Government Printing Office, 1977.

_____. March 1975. Washington, D.C.: U.S. Government Printing Office, 1975.

Johnston, J. *Econometric Methods,* second edition. New York: McGraw-Hill Book Company, 1972.

Keesing, Donald B. "Labor Skills and International Trade: Evaluating Many Trade Flows with a Single Measuring Device." *Review of Economics and Statistics* 47, 3 (August 1965).

Kenen, Peter B., ed. *International Trade and Finance: Frontiers for Research.* Cambridge: Cambridge University Press, 1975.

Kilpatrick, Robert W. "The Validity of the Average Concentration Ratio as a Measure of Industry Structure." *Southern Economic Journal* 42, 4 (April 1976).

_____ . "The Choice Among Alternative Measures of Industrial Concentration." *Review of Economics and Statistics* 49 (April 1967).

Kmenta, Jan. *Elements of Econometrics.* New York: The MacMillan Company, 1971.

Knickerbocker, Frederick T. *Oligopolistic Reaction and Multinational Enterprise.* Boston: Division of Research, Graduate School of Business Administration, Harvard University, 1973.

Leontief, Wassily W. "Domestic Production and Foreign Trade: The American Capital Position Re-examined." *Economia Internazionale* 7, 1 (February 1954).

Lowinger, Thomas C., "The Technology Factor and the Export Performance of U.S. Manufacturing Industries." *Economic Inquiry* 13, 2 (June 1975).

Mann, H. Michael. "Seller Concentration, Barriers to Entry, and Rates of Return in Thirty Industries, 1950-1960." *Review of Economics and Statistics* 48, 3 (August 1966).

Masson, Robert T., and P. David Qualls, eds. *Essays on Industrial Organization in Honor of Joe S. Bain.* Cambridge, Mass.: Ballinger Publishing Company, 1976.

Morrall, John F., III. *Human Capital, Technology, and the Role of the United States in International Trade.* Gainesville: University of Florida Press, 1972.

Mueller, Dennis C., and John E. Tilton. "Research and Development Costs as a Barrier to Entry." Canadian Journal of Economics 2, 4 (November 1969).

National Science Foundation. *Industrial R & D Funds in Relation to Other Economic Variables,* NSF 64-25. Washington, D.C.: National Science Foundation, 1964.

Naya, Seiji. "Natural Resources, Factor Mix, and Factor Reversal in International Trade." *American Economic Review* 57, 2 (May 1967).

Nelson, Ralph L. *Concentration in the Manufacturing Industries of the United States.* New Haven: Yale University Press, 1963.

Ohlin, Bertil. *Interregional and International Trade.* Cambridge, Mass.: Harvard University Press, 1933.

Ophir, Tsvi. "The Interaction of Tariffs and Quotas." *American Economic Review* 59, 5 (December 1969).

Organization for Economic Cooperation and Development. *Gaps in Technology: Electronic Components.* Paris: OECD, 1968.

Pagoulatos, Emilio, and Robert Sorensen. "Domestic Market Structure and International Trade: An Empirical Analysis." *Quarterly Review of Economics and Business* 16, 1 (Spring 1976).

_____ . "International Trade, International Investment and Industrial Profitability of U.S. Manufacturing." *Southern Economic Journal* 42, 3 (January 1976).

_____ . "Two-Way International Trade: An Econometric Analysis." *Weltwirtschaftliches Archiv* 111, 3 (1975).

Peck, Merton J. *Competition in the Aluminum Industry 1945-1958.* Cambridge, Mass.: Harvard University Press, 1961.

Porter, Michael E. *Interbrand Choice, Strategy, and Bilateral Market Power.* Cambridge, Mass.: Harvard University Press, 1976.

_____. "Consumer Behavior, Retailer Power and Market Performance in Consumer Goods Industries." *Review of Economics and Statistics* 56, 4 (November 1974).

Pugel, Thomas A. "Profitability, Concentration, and the Interindustry Variation in Wages." New York University Faculty of Business Administration Working Paper No. 78-84, July 1978.

_____. "Quota Imposition Output, and Monopoly." New York University Faculty of Business Administration Working Paper No. 78-83, July 1978.

Qualls, P. David. "Stability and Persistence of Economic Profit Margins in Highly Concentrated Industries." *Southern Economic Journal* 40, 4 (April 1974).

_____. "Concentration, Barriers to Entry and Long Run Economic Profit Margins." *Journal of Industrial Economics* 20, 2 (April 1972).

Scherer, F.M. *Industrial Market Structure and Economic Performance.* Chicago: Rand McNally Publishing Company, 1970.

_____. "Market Structure and the Employment of Scientists and Engineers." *American Economic Review* 57, 3 (June 1967).

_____, Alan Beckenstein, Erich Kaufer, and R. Dennis Murphy. *The Economics of Multi-Plant Operation.* Cambridge, Mass.: Harvard University Press, 1975.

Schwartzman, David, and Joan Bodoff. "Concentration in Regional and Local Industries." *Southern Economic Journal* 37, 3 (January 1971).

Shepherd, William G. *Market Power and Economic Welfare.* New York: Random House, 1970.

Siegfried, John J. "In Defense of the Average Concentration Ratio." *Journal of Political Economy* 83, 6 (December 1975).

Stonebraker, Robert J. "Corporate Profits and the Risk of Entry." *Review of Economics and Statistics* 58, 1 (February 1978).

Strickland, Allyn D., and Leonard W. Weiss. "Advertising, Concentration, and Price-Cost Margins." *Journal of Political Economy* 84, 5 (October 1976).

Theil, Henri. *Principles of Econometrics.* New York: John Wiley and Sons, 1971.

Throop, Adrian W. "The Union-Nonunion Wage Differential and Cost-Push Inflation." *American Economic Review* 58, 1 (March 1968).

Tilton, John E. *International Diffusion of Technology: The Case of Semiconductors.* Washington, D.C.: The Brookings Institution, 1971.

Travis, William P. "Production, Trade, and Protection When There Are Many Commodities and Two Factors." *American Economic Review* 62, 1 (March 1972).

U.S. Bureau of the Census. *Schedule A: Rates of Duty and Tariff Paragraphs.* Washington, D.C.: U.S. Government Printing Office, 1976.

_____. *Statistical Abstract of the United States: 1971.* Washington, D.C.: U.S. Government Printing Office, 1971.

U.S. Department of Justice, Antitrust Division. *Antitrust Guide for International Operations.* Washington, D.C.: U.S. Government Printing Office, 1977.

Vernon, Raymond. "International Investment and International Trade in the Product Cycle." *Quarterly Journal of Economics* 80, 2 (May 1966).

Walter, Ingo. "Non-Tariff Protection Among Industrial Countries: Some Preliminary Evidence." *Economia Internazionale* 25, 2 (May 1972).

Webbink, Douglas W. *The Semiconductor Industry: A Survey of Structure, Conduct, and Performance.* Washington, D.C.: Federal Trade Commission, Bureau of Economics, 1977.

Weiser, Lawrence, and Keith Jay. "Determinants of the Commodity Structure of U.S. Trade: Comment." *American Economic Review* 62, 3 (June 1972).

Weiss, Leonard W. "The Geographic Size of Markets in Manufacturing." *Review of Economics and Statistics* 54, 3 (August 1972).

_____ . "Advertising, Profits, and Corporate Taxes." *Review of Economics and Statistics* 51, 4 (November 1969).

_____ . "Concentration and Labor Earnings." *American Economic Review* 56, 1 (March 1966).

Wells, Louis T., Jr. "Test of a Product Cycle Model of International Trade: U.S. Exports of Consumer Durables." *Quarterly Journal of Economics* 83, 1 (February 1969).

Williamson, Oliver E. "Managerial Discretion and Business Behavior." New York: John Wiley and Sons, 1971.

Index

About the Author

Thomas A. Pugel is an Assistant Professor of Economics and International Business at New York University Graduate School of Business Administration. He received a B.A. in Economics from Michigan State University and a Ph.D. in Economics from Harvard University. His research interests include industrial organization, international trade, and international taxation. He received the Danielian Award in International Economics from the Department of Economics at Harvard University in 1975.